Frank Brank

Follow Me

Christian Discipleship for Today

By John M. Drescher

HERALD PRESS, SCOTTDALE, PENNSYLVANIA

To my parents
Who in many small and meaningful ways showed me
the way of Christian discipleship.

Follow Me

This volume of meditations is for the modern disciple. The meditations cover a wide selection of subjects which are of a common concern to Christ's disciples. They are meant to help, to strengthen, or simply encourage the modern disciple.

The author points up what Christian commitment involves in today's world. Time and again the disparity between mere churchianity and true Christianity is revealed. The author is positive and pulls you out of a passive posture. You will be stirred to practice New Testament discipleship.

What does it take to really make a disciple? Discipleship is Christianity in practice. Discipleship displays that Christianity has a purpose for today. Discipleship recognizes Jesus as Lord and Master in everyday events. It is "Thy will be done on earth as it is in heaven."

Discipleship is the daily call of Christ, "Come learn of me." It is not a once for all commitment but a constant commitment to Christ's will in all of life's relationships. Christ is the way for going, the truth for knowing, and the life for living.

"The disciple is dragged out of his relative security into a life of absolute insecurity. From a life which is observable and calculable into a life where everything is unobservable and fortuitous, out of the realm of finite and into the realm of infinite possibilities." So wrote Bonhoeffer, one of Christ's modern-day disciples.

In the farewell speech of old Mr. Standfast in *Pilgrim's Progress* just before he crossed the river he said: "I have loved to hear my Lord spoken of and wherever I have seen the print of His shoe in the earth, I have coveted to set my foot." This is the desire and the duty of every disciple of the Lord as Peter says: "Indeed this is your calling. For Christ suffered for you and left you a personal example, and wants you to follow in his steps."*

The life of the disciple is not a life of rules or a set of principles. Discipleship means obedience to Jesus Christ in His constant call, FOLLOW ME.

"As he [Jesus] went along, he saw Levi, son of Alphaeus at his seat in the custom-house, and said to him, 'Follow me'; and Levi rose and followed him."° °

°From *The New Testament in Modern English,* © J. B. Phillips, 1950. Used by permission of The Macmillan Company.

° °From *The New English Bible.* © The Delegates of the Oxford University Press and the Syndics of the Cambridge University Press, 1961, 1970. Used by permission.

Contents

1. Just Tell Me

Richard C. Raines, well-known writer and bishop of the Methodist Church, illustrated a prevalent spiritual attitude by reading a letter of a child which said: "Dear God, what is it like when you die? Nobody will tell me. I just want to know. I don't want to do it." Bishop Raines commented, "We tend to be that way spiritually. 'O God, what is it like to be converted? I don't want to do it. I just want to know about it.' "

Raines' remark is a good reminder. Sometimes I think we've prayed and written enough about renewal, revival, repentance, race, and reaching our neighbors for Christ. It seems the Lord may see us simply standing still and praying, "O God, send renewal and revival.

Bring men to repentance and restore right race relations. O God, we pray for the poor. Please save our neighbors and send missionaries. But we don't want to do it. We want to pretend we are pious in praying like this."

We many times manage to accomplish what a deacon, who got his metaphors mixed, prayed: "Lord, send a mighty fire of revival. And, Lord, whenever there is one small spark, water that spark." We pray for God to do a new work, but whenever we see that it might involve us or see someone else being used or blessed, we pour water on the whole idea.

Without a doubt one of the great needs is to live according to the light we have. It is not only to learn about the truth but to live the truth. It is not only to discern what the need is but to do all within our power to meet the need. True prayer always puts legs under the person who prays. It is utter deceit to pray for something we know we will not receive.

Renewal and radiant living result when we begin to pray, "O God, what is it like to be converted? Make me a demonstration. What is it like to repent? As You show me, I promise to turn from every evil way. What is it like to share the gospel? I commit myself to be Your evangel, be it for life or death."

12

2. Need of the Miraculous

"Every fundamental thing in the evangelical faith is challenged today, not in the world, but in the church. The whole mentality of our generation rationalizes faith till it has taken out of the Gospel every vital quality and every miracle-working power. Yet the church that does not work miracles is dead and ought to be buried," said Chadwick many years ago shortly before his death.

This sounds as if it were written today. With a world in need of a divine demonstration of power and miracle-working, many are content to be concerned with religiosity. Others spend too much time merely questioning the miraculous in Christianity or denying it altogether.

David K. Wachtel reminds us that the town Trier, which was the hometown of Karl Marx, boasted that it had more religious buildings than any other town its size in Europe. The fact was, however, in spite of all its front of religious activities, Christianity was dead.

"Theologians of the era prided themselves in their critical study of the Scriptures — spending lifetimes chewing little morsels of doubt. They seemed to glorify themselves rather than Christ. A cross, a fountain filled with blood, an empty tomb, a love divine, grace unlimited, and simple faith to appropriate all this were lost in a cloudy shroud of doubt."

No wonder Wachtel continues, "Men who wrap themselves in questions and doubt *cannot* crusade! Who will risk all — who would die — for a question mark? . . . Religion becomes 'opium' and the failure of the church produced a Karl Marx, an Adolf Hitler — or their . . . successors!"

There is always the danger, in every generation, that we turn to secondary things. Paul warned the Christians at Colossae, "Beware lest any man spoil you through philosophy and vain deceit, after the tradition of men, after the rudiments of the world, and not after Christ" (Colossians 2:8).

Every generation is tempted to set itself to admiring brilliant and critical minds and philosophies until faith in Christ and the miraculous is gone, the stakes are removed rather than strengthened, and only ramshackle doubt remains. There is not enough believed to become explicit or excited about. And doubts, arising from cold hearts and disbelief more than from intellectual difficulties, drive back truth, hope, and confidence.

Then it is that we turn to secondary concerns. We become crusaders for many things "not after Christ." Doubt drives out the miraculous in Christ. Lesser concerns are enlarged to fill the vacuum.

But we have a message of great affirmations. The Christian life is based upon the miraculous and great certainties. If there is to be real renewal, we must dwell on these great affirmations and certainties of our faith. We must believe our beliefs and doubt our doubts rather than believe our doubts and doubt our beliefs.

To do this takes a definite and clear knowledge of the Word of God. Therefore study of, trust in, and obedience to, the Word of God will always be paramount in bringing about renewal, in building morality, faith, and truth.

Confidence in the Scriptures must be strengthened and not weakened. Every Christian must be led into the study and obedience of Scripture for spiritual sustenance and growth. We must believe in the miraculous and expect God to work miracles today. Else we are dead and ought to be buried.

3. Plea for Passion

I'm putting in a plea for passion. I do not mean sentimentalism (Christianity is never sentimental), but an intensiveness, earnestness, and enthusiasm which live the life of God and present the great truths of God in such a way as to move men for God. Passion is not some reaction without reason but only a reasonable response to God's greatness and goodness to the point where we not only know it ourselves but show it and let others know it.

We are too calm and cool in living the Christian life. We know the facts intellectually, yet often with little spiritual warmth. We live with a kind of passiveness which begets nothing. Great truths are gone over so glibly it sometimes seems irreverent to say them again.

17

But why be concerned with passion? Why be so much in earnest? Why get emotional at all about the Christian life?

When there is no passion, there is no persuasion. We witness this in many worship services. Where there is little intensiveness, there is little interest. We see it in many lives. Where there is little emotion, there is little energy exerted even for a good thing. We experience this in many areas. We do not move others until we ourselves are moved.

What happens? Because of little passion we pass to poor substitutes. These are easily seen.

We may depend upon dogmatism. We try to teach the truth our way in an arrogant manner. Holy passion is gone, but our position must be held and we attempt to do this by being dogmatic.

When divine passion is lacking, we may take to fanaticism. It's a poor substitute. Fanaticism shows itself in excessive enthusiasm, often over some finite concern or issue, and in its unreasoning zeal. The fanatic blows up one small thing while freely skipping over important concerns. When the warmth of spiritual passion is gone, it isn't hard to get hot over something peripheral.

Then, too, passion can be replaced (particularly today) by mere intellectualism. No, passion and intellectualism are not exclusive of each other. True passion is based on knowledge. But there is an intellectualism which delights to put everything in precise and perfect phrases backed by bounteous research and study yet leaving the hearers cold. It is as heartless, harmless, and hopeless as it desires to be dignified and delightful. It can become a substitute for the knowledge of God and His will. Passion burns warm in the heart which comes only through personal application of the Word and prayer.

A lack of passion may push one to another extreme called emotionalism. This "whipped up" type of experience of the moment can never suffice. To some it may give a sense of reality. It is only a substitute and a poor one.

Ceremonialism can be an attempt to replace divine passion and devotion. Right ceremony and ritual are always in order. True reverence is never out of date. But in a day of great love for liturgy we dare not be deceived into thinking that approaching God by certain forms, ritual, or liturgy we deserve or receive His blessing. Stress upon ceremony may be a substitute for hearts without passion.

All this calls me to put in a plea for passion

— a passion or spiritual enthusiasm which flows from a warm personal and abiding walk with God, a spiritual touch and insight springing from Holy Spirit illumination of the Word and prayer until God's Word burns in the heart, a spiritual glow seen and known by others, and a love for men which never stops with mere words and methods of soul-winning but which actually leads men to Christ.

True spiritual passion by no means pleads for ignorance or sentimentality. It calls for the greatest intellectual grasp of God and His will. It demands a positive position. It is the spiritual warmth which draws others from a cold world to the bosom of Christ. It is the spiritual practice which permeates the life with secret prayer and not only talks about prayer. It is the spiritual glow which goes with obedience to God. It is the spiritual knowledge which finds the Word sweeter than honey. It is that which goes beyond the mere spoken word and out of its own internal quality and concern draws men to God.

This kind of passion cannot be worked up. It cannot be man-made if it is missing. It cannot be missed if it is present. It comes freely from the hand of God to those who know constant prayer, obedience, and God's indwelling love.

4. Signs of Maturity

A small boy was asked why he fell out of bed. He replied, "I guess I slept too close to the place I got in."

That tells the story of many persons. Because they did not advance after becoming Christians their lives were filled with "fallings." The Scripture speaks of laying aside childish habits and becoming mature. The growing Christian avoids many pitfalls.

Here are a few signs of spiritual maturity.

Love which goes on loving in spite of suffering, disappointment, and heartache is a sign of maturity. Love which is large enough to include all persons, which doesn't depend on honor, recognition, or favors, is the love that comes from maturity.

Joy is a sign of spiritual maturity. To be joyful through discouraging or adverse circumstances is maturity, for joy depends on a relationship while happiness depends on what happens.

Peace is a sign of spiritual maturity. This is the ability to suffer wrong rather than to be wrong. The easy way of slapping back when mistreated is childish and immature. Maturity is in going the second mile and turning the other cheek. To be a peacemaker is to be mature.

To be long-suffering is to be mature. This is patience under pressure. Here is where we are usually tested by others. It depends on how much of God we have on the inside as to how much pressure we can stand on the outside.

Gentleness is a sign of spiritual maturity. This is the spirit which remains kind when there is every reason to retaliate or respond angrily. It is the gentle spirit and word in response to the unruly or to the irritations of life. It would rather be hurt than to hurt.

A mature person demonstrates goodness. Goodness is generosity in things material and in things spiritual. It is to be courteous, sympathetic, considerate, and of constant benefit to others.

Faith is a sign of spiritual maturity. To trust

others and to be trustworthy, to have an unswerving trust in God and faithfulness in fulfilling our responsibilities, is to be mature.

A mature person is meek. Meekness means that one is able to control his strength and speech because his confidence is in God. Meekness makes one willing to take a lower place than one deserves, to be silent about one's merits, to bear slights, insults, and false accusation for "Christ's sake."

One who is mature exercises self-control. He weighs what is best and abstains from the rest. He knows how to sacrifice the lesser for the higher good, how to discern between good and evil and take the good.

These are sure signs of maturity. And lo, they are the fruits of the Spirit. It is only as we give ourselves to the Spirit's control that we can grow into maturity.

5. Pentecost's Product

At Pentecost the Holy Spirit came to man in fulfillment of promise, with a new purpose and with a new power. Men were changed. Life took on a new perspective and was filled with divine energy. The Book of Acts points to the importance of Pentecost. Without Pentecost there would be no "Acts" to write about. No wonder then that Pentecost is placed at the very beginning of the book.

On Pentecost, occurring fifty days after the resurrection of Christ and ten days after His ascension, the Holy Spirit was poured out upon a company of 120 believers in an upper room in Jerusalem. The Holy Spirit came to abide with and in the church. Jesus promised in John 14:16, 17, "And I will pray the Father, and he shall give you another Comforter, that he may abide with you for ever; even the Spirit of truth; whom the world cannot receive, because it seeth him not, neither knoweth him: but ye know him; for he dwelleth with you, and shall be in you."

In the Old Testament, the Spirit came and went, but did not abide and remain. He came upon certain individuals to equip and prepare them for special service and office. The coming of the Spirit at Pentecost was different. He came to stay, dwelling in the body of Christ and in the individual believer.

But what did Pentecost produce? It produced empowered people. Jesus had promised power after the coming of the Holy Spirit. Now there was personal power to stand the storms of persecution and to meet the hours of martyrdom.

There was also power in prayer. Their words had power because they were prompted by the Holy Spirit. The sightless saw, the deaf heard, the dumb spoke, and the lame walked.

They preached with great power. The rebellious repented, the multitudes were moved, and the doubters could doubt no longer. Why? Because God's people presented themselves to God in such a way that the power of the

Holy Spirit pulsated through their entire personality. And this Person and Power is ours today if we will yield to Him with the same abandonment of Pentecost.

Pentecost also produces witnesses. From Pilate's palace, through Roman roads, to the end of the empire they witnessed to Christ's glorious resurrection. In homes and streets and synagogues they spoke of what they had seen and heard. Wonder filled the people's minds, willingness for God characterized the believers' hearts, and witnessing flowed from the disciples' lips.

Further, none could question the reality of revelation of such witnessing. For in its wake lay changed lives. Abandoned sin, broken habits, and deserted idols proved it was the truth they told. People saw and felt a new source of strength. Barriers were broken down. Love replaced fear and distrust. All those who believed found a great unity. While the witnesses could not but speak the things they had seen and heard, the world could not but believe that what it heard and saw was God living among men. The Spirit of God was come.

Today the call of Christ is just as clear. The challenge to us is just as constant. The world is waiting for Christ's words. The Spirit is here to empower us to witness. Christ, proclaimed, will win despite the seriousness of sin.

Pentecost produced grace-filled people. "And with great power gave the apostles witness of the resurrection of the Lord Jesus: and great grace was upon them all" (Acts 4:33). Few had great finance. The disciples were not persons of prominence or position. Perhaps there was even a shortage of talents and abilities, but there was an abundance of grace.

The experiences of God's grace made them gracious. God's saving, sanctifying, satisfying, and sustaining grace made burden bearing and cross bearing take on a new perspective. It imparted radiant peace and joy. They met temptations and trial with grace which the non-Christian could not gainsay. The gift of God's grace was to them a pardon for the past and a pattern for the present. It gave desire and hope for the future.

God's grace is not gone, nor has it diminished. Many times it is not appropriated. Where God's Spirit abides and reigns, is great grace — to save, to sanctify, to satisfy, to sustain, and to impart this same grace to others.

6. Aglow with the Spirit

Some years ago Dean Inge prophesied, "The future will show whether civilization, as we know it, can be amended or must be ended. The time seems ripe for a new birth of religious and spiritual life, which may remold society, as no less potent force would have strength to do."

Today many are raising the same question in one form or another. Can our civilization be mended or must it be ended? There is the repeated reminder also of the ripeness of our time for real revival. Moral and spiritual values must change if there is to be a future. This will come about through the recognition and power of the Divine.

It is significant then that Hugh T. Kerr, Jr.,

28

wrote a dozen or so years ago, "It is surely more than a coincidence that the ineffectiveness of the Christian witness in our day has gone hand in hand with a tragic neglect of the doctrine of the Holy Spirit and a consequent dimming of the victorious radiance of the Christian life."

One often hears it said that the doctrine of the Spirit is today the most neglected of all the doctrines of the Christian faith. Multitudes, as in Paul's day, have never heard that there is a Holy Spirit.

In one of his "Miscellanies" Thomas Carlyle asks: "How did Christianity rise and spread abroad among men?"

He answers: "It arose in the mystic depths of man's soul and it spread abroad by the preaching of the Word . . . and it flew like hallowed fire from heart to heart, till all whom it touched were purified and illuminated by its power."

Today we are struggling with method. We organize great programs for evangelism. It is good to remind ourselves occasionally that the Spirit of evangelism is far, far more important than the method. Carlyle indicates the essential characteristic of an evangelistic witness. We are called to preach the Word, that is, testify to Christ. This testimony is what we ourselves know of Him through personal experience. That witness is to be not through our own gimmicks or power of personality but in the power of God's Spirit. Notice the relevance of Paul's injunction, "Be aglow with the Spirit" (Romans 12:11). "Where there is no warmth there can be no light."

So it is that always where we fulfill the primary task of evangelism, life is marked by the presence, power, and glow of the Spirit. The Spirit changes us from the conventional, indulgent, unheroic life so common today and reproduces again in our lives what the Savior is.

The characteristic of the Christian is to possess Christlike qualities of life. The overwhelming realization of the presence and power of the living Christ in the early church made a mighty evangelistic impulse that swept across seas and through history. It can do the same today.

Always at the heart of faithful ambassadors is a spiritual glow. There is nothing of a musty mediocrity and fear of being fools for Christ's sake. The test of the Christian life then is really the possession of the Spirit. "If any man have not the Spirit of Christ, he is none of his." The Holy Spirit living, yes, reigning in the lives of people places a glow of light, love, and joy in which the Spirit can lift the fallen, help the erring, and melt the hardened heart. The light of the Holy Spirit cannot be hidden from our faces.

So it is that we must always go beyond technique, organization, and program to see that our work is essentially witness to Christ in the power of the Spirit who moves "like hallowed fire from heart to heart."

"Come, Holy Spirit, Heav'nly Dove,
　　With all Thy quick'ning pow'rs;
Kindle a flame of sacred love
　　In these cold hearts of ours."

7. What Is Needed?

At times I suppose each of us becomes concerned that with all the preaching and teaching going on today so few real changes are taking place. Sermons are preached but no visible change appears in the lives of the hearers. Sunday school classes and other Bible groups are taught but a feeling of spiritual hunger and inadequacy continues. Why the spiritual dryness in the center of so much spiritual work?

Consider these two requirements if real spiritual work is to be done. First, complete, concrete, unreserved commitment of self is required. This is true for the advancement of any cause. It is an absolute necessity in order for God to work and manifest Himself to anyone.

Now it is true, as someone suggested, that

the devil will let us do many good things so long as we reserve a part of ourselves for ourselves. The devil will allow us to preach, to teach, to give in abundance of our material blessings, to seek to witness, to pray, to read our Bibles regularly, and to be good and kind so long as we do not surrender unconditionally to Jesus Christ. The devil knows his work is doomed by complete dedication to Jesus. We might as well confess that right here.

What does it mean to have complete dedication? It means that we say regarding everything in life, "Not my will, but Thine." It means that we not only give lip service to Christ's lordship but that we really step by step are led by His Spirit; that we pull out all the stops; that we say "yes" to all Christ asks of us and "no" to all which displeases Him.

Second, if a real spiritual work is to be done, there must be the clear and conscious enablement of the Holy Spirit. Charles Haddon Spurgeon years ago wrote about the preaching which kills. It still stands true today. Notice what he said.

"The preaching that kills may be, and often is, orthodox — dogmatically, inviolably orthodox. In the Christian system, unction is the anointing of the Holy Ghost, separating a person unto God's work, and preparing him for it. This unction is the one divine enablement by which the preacher accomplishes the peculiar and saving ends of preaching. Without this unction there are no true spiritual results accomplished. The results and forces in preaching do not rise above the results of unsanctified speech. Without unction the former is as potent as the pulpit . . . without it the gospel has no more power to propagate itself than any other system of truth. This is the seal of its divinity. Unction in the preacher puts God in the gospel."

How we need to hear this! We too much operate today as if teaching, preaching, and persuading in themselves will bring in the kingdom and change persons. We think if we just do a little bit more ourselves we'll see persons and things changed. God, on the other hand, says, "All is vain unless the Spirit." God says a little with the blessing of the Spirit results in the salvation of many, but no amount of effort without His blessing avails. May God help us not only to see the need of complete commitment and Holy Spirit enablement but to really yield until no one will doubt that the living God is among us.

34

8. Parable of the Other

It came to pass that a certain missionary and his family went to a far country to seek souls for the Savior. Now it was not easy, the culture being different, the language difficult, and the living at times dangerous. But these things were not nearly so difficult to bear as when the natives whispered and lied about the missionaries and stole their goods. This I say was hard for them to take and keep on loving the people. In fact, the missionary seemingly could not take it. When someone stole from him, he began to avoid that person. If one lied to him or whispered about him, he simply could not love him but rather ignored him from that day on.

Because of his attitude, the mission board

called him home. Upon hearing it, the home folks, those of his home church, gossiped such things as, "Didn't he know before he left that missionaries must love the unlovely? What's wrong with him? The person who lies and steals is the very person who needs his help most." "He should have done everything to get next to those people spiritually rather than avoiding them when they stole from him." And with many other such expressions did they speak one to another.

Now it happened that in that same church there were many fine orthodox families. There were also nearby others who were unsaved, whom the pastor was laboring hard to win. It was known that these sometimes lied, even stole. And so it came to pass on a certain night that one whom the pastor and other saints were seeking to help to Christ stole a small item from a member of the church (at least it was reported so). Even worse, it seemed he lied about taking it. Ah, that was hard. What should be done?

This is what was done. From that day the soul that needed help, the soul who stole and lied, was avoided. "If he is in it, if he is going along, I'm out," said the church member. "If that's the way he acts, the best one can do is to stay as far from him as possible." "Don't give him a chance to get you again." And with many other expressions did they speak one to another. And thus the one who needed help most, the one, of all people, who should not have been avoided, the one whom the pastor was seeking to see saved by the Savior, was driven further from Christ. And who shall reap the judgment of God?

Then it came to pass that one stepped forward and asked, "Pastor, what meaneth this parable? Make it even plainer."

And the pastor said, "The meaning of the parable is this: The one who lies and steals and cheats is unsaved, no matter where in the world he lives. It is always easier, when the love of God is lacking, to give money to support a missionary who is to love and win those who lie and steal in some distant land than it is to love one who lies and steals at home. Love for Christ and the lost is tested more in how we treat our unsaved neighbor than by our giving and praying for the lost in Africa and China.

"One who is a foreign missionary and lacks love is soon spotted and perhaps even sent home, but what shall be done for the home member? Let it be known that one who cannot love in the surroundings of a Christian community is a far worse sinner. Let such an individual repent and pray for Calvary love, lest his life come under the terrible judgment of God and that speedily."

9. Beneath the Surface

Jesus had a way of speaking to the need of man which is beneath the surface — to man's real need. This is what the true teacher of God must do to be faithful today. It is easy to talk about the prevailing, popular problems of man. Through the centuries it has been all too common that the church has only mouthed what had already caught the attention of the world. Christ saw deeper. So must we.

While men raved about Roman rule and longed for release, Jesus spoke of Satan's rule and led persons to new and lasting freedom. While men spoke of the greatness of power, Jesus spoke of the greatness of patience. While men spoke of honor, Jesus spoke of the blessings of humility. While men spoke of the beauty of the temple, Jesus spoke of the beauty of holiness.

While men spoke of the sinfulness and separateness of the Samaritans, Jesus spoke of the struggle and salvation of man's soul. While men spoke of religion, Jesus spoke of renewal of the heart of man. Men spoke of mighty armies. Jesus spoke of the power of faith, though it be small as a grain of mustard seed. Men spoke of Caesar's military might. Jesus spoke of the power of love. While men spoke of the magnificence of Rome, Jesus spoke of the majesty of God, seen in the sky and the flowers.

Yes, Jesus always saw beneath the surface to where the real struggle of man goes on. He knew that the inner life of man must be renewed before we can really speak of renewal of society. He knew that people must be born again before they can live like new creatures. He knew that inner struggles of the soul must be overcome before right relationships with others can be established.

So also the spiritual leader has an insight which sees beneath man's outward appearance. Of course we cannot avoid social, economic, and other common concerns of all men. No doubt, however, today's search for outer space is indicative of the inner search for help outside ourselves. The struggle for freedom politically or socially, which every man seeks, cannot be seen fully outside of the deeper struggle for freedom which goes on in his own soul. The separation we see in the ghettos men build is indicative also of the separation we experience between ourselves and God in our own souls.

Man's search for security through an over-abundance of things, insurances, bank accounts, and health plans reveals, without a doubt, his great inner insecurity and his sense of need of divine satisfaction. Man's mania for materialism today is certainly an effort to fill the vacuum he feels in his own life. Man needs love. The indulgence in all kinds of lust today points to the lack of love felt in many hearts.

So one can go on and on, and the closer we come to Christ, the more we can see that His concern for man always cuts to the core of man's problems. He saw beneath the surface. So must we.

10. Close the Performance Gap

Many times I'm struck by the safety of doctrine; that is, as long as it is not related directly to life. Preach all you want to on the first eleven chapters of Romans. The protest begins when the practical outcome is pressed in Romans twelve through fifteen.

Preach sin as long as you relate it to Adam's fall, the world, and the sin of the fathers, keeping it as far back as Abraham, Isaac, and Jacob. Describe, in any church group, the doctrine of the devil in great detail. But beware of suggesting that the devil is doing his dirty work when we sow discord among brethren, when we gossip, and when we despise others. Trouble begins if present-day sins are spoken about in the lives of God's people today.

So also the doctrine of God is safe. But to apply that doctrine of God to the point where He says He will allow no other gods before Him or that He must have total claim on life means trouble. The doctrine of Christ is safe, especially if His deity, virgin birth, and coming again are spoken of properly. This is right, for one can't develop right living from wrong doctrine. All kinds of protests are put forth by the most orthodox if the way of Christ is pushed to the point the Scripture does when it says Christ is Lord as well as Savior.

Take the example of the doctrine of love. We may preach loud and long on love, brotherhood, and God's love for the world. But when we begin to apply the doctrine the way the Scripture does, we are immediately in hot water. To even suggest, as Christ commands, that one is to love his enemies, to pray for the enemies in wartime, and to give to or to sympathize with both sides in conflict causes cries of communist, traitor, and liberal.

When we are told to love those who differ from us, the cry goes up that we are compromising and that the Scripture calls us to "come out from among them." To suggest that we ought to love and forbear even with brethren who do differently than we do or think, causes some to raise a question mark over one's own head. In the minds of some, Paul could not have been Christian and called the believers at Corinth "saints."

Yet nowhere in Scripture are Christians told to come out from among other Christians. The Scriptures speak only of Christians coming out from the world's evil, from idol worshipers and those committed to evil.

So it is safe, very safe, to speak on doctrine, to repeat the Apostles' Creed, and to sing songs of love and praise. The real problem for any preacher or writer begins where the Scripture is applied to life, right where we put in our working hours, our playing time, and make our gritty decisions each day.

It is at the point of doctrine's application to life that sharp criticisms sometimes come. Here voices cry social gospel and give us more of the plain simple gospel and more Scripture verses.

Doctrine is worthless and only an intellectual exercise unless it makes a difference in life. It doesn't matter how high a person jumps in spiritual ecstasy if it doesn't determine how he walks in relation to his fellowmen. Christianity begins where talk stops and the action begins.

Will we close the performance gap — the gap between what we say and do?

A generation or two ago we went through a mood of sophisticated indecision. There was the great fear of fanaticism. Professors and preachers straddled the fence on nearly every issue. To believe anything strongly was thought stupid. With this spirit of sophisticated indecision the call to commitment died. We feared speaking out on anything. Commitment meant merely to raise the hand or go through an instruction period and we were in to stay.

Now we must hear again that decisive commitment is demanded. The only way to further light is to live boldly for the truth which we understand now.

To close the performance gap demands that deeds equal words and faith is expressed in works. To be sure, we will experience persecution first from those who through the past decades were satisfied with a religion which decided little and demanded less.

Only when we yield in decision and commitment to the idea that Christ deserves and demands absolute loyalty and has something to say about every area of life will we close the performance gap.

11. Who Is a Prophet?

How do we recognize a prophet? History points out how difficult a problem it is. It is difficult, first of all, because a prophet usually appears from a place different from what we expect. We expect him to come with the credentials of good background, education, and official status, not out of Nazareth.

More than once God stepped down to pull a man from the plow or out of poverty and put him on a high pulpit as His prophet. More than once the one having nobility of figure or royal background has stepped forward only to have God say, "Not this one. Is there yet another?"

This is hard for us to see. We stone the prophets even as our forefathers did. Today we clap for Bunyan even though we, like those of his day, would likely not admit the living Bunyan to our fellowship. It is one thing to applaud the prophets of the past and another to perceive who is a prophet in the present.

"Seven towns contend for Homer dead
Through which the living Homer begged
his bread."

Strange as it may sound, throughout history prophets are recognized least by those in leadership — officials, if you please. These gave Christ and all the prophets plenty of trouble. As Alexander Maclaren wrote: "It is a terrible thing for any man to be official. He is no longer himself — his natural, free, frank, fresh, general, original self; he is weighed down with something; he is afraid of spectators; he reads the bible of precedent; he studies the apocrypha of tradition. . . . Irregular," says Maclaren, "is a dangerous word in the mouth of officialism."

A true prophet speaks of things bigger than himself and his own pet peeves. Some claim to be prophets and many even sound like prophets yet are wrapped up in their own small program. They are self-defensive. They speak of themselves rather than God. Such are hurt most, not when people turn from God, but when people will not listen to them.

A true prophet preaches both punishment and promise. Pity the person whose prophecy is only one of destruction. A true prophet speaks of repentance and also restoration, of the punishment of the evildoer and the possibilities of the one who turns to God from wrong. He is as long on God's grace for the sinner as on God's hatred of the sin.

A true prophet proclaims God's message with a bleeding heart and with eyes full of tears. He does not desire to damn or destroy others but to draw people to God for repentance and new life.

A true prophet does not prophesy to provide a following for himself; he prophesies God's truth because he feels he must even though no one listens. Too many today, to prove they are right, must organize a group against other groups. The reason for existence is the group's disagreement with other groups.

A true prophet is least concerned about his own glory or lack of glory. He doesn't brag about his backers or attack people merely because they oppose him. All glory goes to God and he knows God is greater than all his adversaries and able to take care of critics.

48

12. Real Worship!

Some time ago I attended America's religious worship service. The congregation was larger than I had ever attended inside any church. It had a definite ritual. The worshipers were most enthusiastic and dedicated. Not even the drizzle dampened the spirits or stopped the service which was held outside. There was rapt attention until the entire worship service was concluded.

Then the congregation went forth as powerful witnesses of all that happened. The next day the message was scattered in every shop, school, and street corner.

But let me describe it in more detail.

I noticed persons who gathered for the worship service were well on time. Some must have called ahead for reserved seats. Ushers were especially careful of such. Few, if any, came late. The front seats were taken first.

When the ritual began, all became very quiet. The leaders of worship stood reverently at attention while the opening song was announced and sung. The audience also stood for the song and faced what might be called the altar. The soloist sang with unmistakable vigor. The offering — well, that was taken as we entered the service. Willingly and without exception each attender gave $5.00.

As the service progressed, I was impressed with the attention of the group. The service lasted approximately two hours. Yet no one wanted to miss any part of it or lost interest in what was going on. In fact, the majority seemed ready to testify at any point in the service how they felt and where they thought the whole service should be improved.

Fellowship was grand. People I never saw before turned to me with friendly faces. At different times some said things like "The weather's just perfect for this," "He's right," or "Wasn't that good?" And many others, I noticed, were very friendly to each other.

Oh, yes, before the main part of the service started, the names of persons on the program were announced. Here is when I noticed the real worship and devotion the attenders experienced. With the announcement of each name the people clapped. You could tell the persons on the program were worshiped by all. I was told the large offerings made possible large salaries for these persons.

During the program a number were assigned to, at times, get up and whip up the congregation; so enthusiasm was kept up. These, about six or eight persons, made all kinds of motions and even jumped into the air at times. Everything on the program must have taken hours and days of serious preparation. I wondered how those in charge got people to take time from their busy schedules to prepare.

Then about halfway through, another part of the ritual was carried out. A large group, who again must have practiced long and hard, provided music and performed in a very striking way before the whole congregation. It was very ritualistic. They marched in a certain way. Music, suitable for the occasion, was played. Those who knew, told me the marching and music was pretty much repetition of what is done in each such service. After a good stretch of this part of the ritual, the second part of the program got under way.

Although the second half was very similar to the first half, and it was now real late, no one seemed to mind. The program was all outside. Water was dripping from umbrellas. And it was getting cold.

Yet no one left his seat. Somehow the religious devotion here was really dramatic — far beyond that which I've ever seen in church. To go through all of this and yet hear not one of the thousands in attendance utter one word of complaint was striking to say the least.

Finally the whole service was over. As a concluding part of the ritual those who performed best were carried off the field. And every one gave a last shout of praise and adoration. Expressions of worship and praise were heard all the way to my car.

Next day it seemed everywhere I went, in the barber shop, in the grocery store, and at work, the truth of the night before had gotten around. It was really the talk of the town. For apparently all who attended the service were turned into real evangelists. Even the city paper carried a complete story of the entire program. The headlines read "Clarion Football Team Wins Another Great One." And the people worshiped all over again.

13. A Different Standard

A stabbingly true-to-life cartoon appearing in two parts is described by Leslie B. Flynn in his book entitled, *Your God and Your Gold*. At the top is the grave of Jim Elliot, one of the missionaries martyred by the Auca Indians. The caption says, "He is no fool who gives what he cannot keep to gain what he cannot lose."

Underneath is a drawing of a modern home with a swimming pool, two late-model cars, large yard with outdoor equipment, two TV sets, and modern furniture. On the patio, sitting in a lounging chair, is a young husband who has just finished reading a letter handed to him by his wife, who stands by his side. They exclaim, "Another missionary appeal. We gave our tithe. Surely no one expects us to give more."

The person who said "it costs so much to live today" wasn't really correct. The one who said "it costs so much to live the way we want to live today" was more honest.

Christians have generally and without question accepted the world's standard of living. What is practiced by the non-Christian in regard to what kind of and how many cars, conveniences, clothes, luxuries, expensive high-fidelity sets, and vacations is unquestionably accepted as the Christian standard.

It is assumed that the Christian can buy and eat all he can afford and give what he will to the cause of Christ. We have at times, by one measure or another, taught people that the tithe (the starting place for Christian giving) is doing one's duty even though living in luxury. The Scriptures teach giving in proportion to the prosperity with which the Lord blesses us. Yet we buy as the Lord prospers. We build as He prospers. We travel and take vacations as He prospers. He still says, "Give as the Lord prospers."

This form of worldliness hasn't hit us hard enough. The fact is, we haven't heard much about it. We have adopted a worldly standard of evaluation and practice. In the stewardship of life, a most basic area of the whole Christian life, we live not by the Christian standard but by the same standard the unsaved follow. We "walk as men."

What am I saying? First of all, that in taking Christ as Savior and Lord and entering His kingdom, we live by a different standard. When we accept the call of Christ to salvation, He asks for our all. To be separate means a stewardship of life which strikes the path of "strangers and pilgrims." Some must build mansions because they have hope of none beyond this life. But we dare never settle down to such an extent that should the Lord suddenly want us elsewhere, we find ourselves immovable.

Further, we dare never feel that having given a portion of our pay (regardless of how liberal), the rest is ours to do with as we will. We must always realize that, regardless of how richly rewarded we are, we are not blessed to keep but always to give. To have more, means not to measure more for ourselves but as the Lord prospered to give more for Christ's cause. The Christian can never console himself by thinking that having given liberally the Lord allows him the luxury of what is left.

Finally, living by a standard different from the world means we scrutinize seriously the purchases we make and the possessions we have. It means we find our contentment, not in things or possessions here, but in being good stewards, as those who look for their Lord's return and as those who are always ready to move on.

14. Why Nations Fall

I suppose the part of Edward Gibbon's monumental work, *The Decline and Fall of the Roman Empire*, which is referred to most is the section which gives what he calls the five basic reasons why the great Roman civilization withered and died.

First, a basic reason for the fall of the Roman Empire, he lists, "The undermining of the dignity and sanctity of the home, which is the basis for human society." We have always been told that the church, community, and nation are as strong as the homes. Forces against a stable home today are many. Although there certainly are many fine homes, yet something is drastically wrong in a nation where one in four marriages ends in divorce and where, in addition to this, many husbands and wives are separated.

Second, Gibbon says, "Higher and higher taxes and the spending of public money for free bread and circuses for the populace" was a main cause for the empire's fall. The great craze on the part of many people to get something for nothing is not a good sign, be it in the grocery store or by legislation in Congress.

Third, "the mad craze for pleasure, sports becoming every year more exciting, more brutal, more immoral" helped lead to Rome's fall. Perhaps at no time in history has such a large part of the population been wrapped up in pleasure and sports. Nothing is spared if it will promise fun and more fun. Some kinds of sports seem almost like a vicarious experience which allows a person to vicariously take it out on the other fellow.

A fourth reason Gibbon lists for the fall of the Roman Empire points directly at our nation. It is "the building of great armaments when the real enemy was within — the decay of individual responsibility." Our nation is certainly showing its insecurity today by the very fact that it seeks so hard to find its security in weapons. The piles of armaments were never so high.

Finally Gibbon writes, Rome fell because of "the decay of religion; faith fading into mere form, losing touch with life, losing power to guide the people." One religious leader said, "Our main problem is not liberalism, nor even neoorthodoxy; that which threatens us is a subtle, objective approach to the Bible, to theology, and to preaching in general, which is unrelated to holy living."

He then goes on to say that audiences sit and listen week by week to preaching without any evidence of transformed character or Spirit-anointed witnessing. The preaching mysteriously lacks the authority of heaven and the relevancy to our times which brings about conviction, repentance, faith, and obedience. We return from so-called Bible conferences without any evidence of having met with God.

Says Stephen Olford, "O that God would teach us that it is just as important to be spiritual as to be sound in our approach to the Bible, just as vital to be obedient as to be orthodox, and that the purpose of revelation is nothing less than transformation of human lives!"

In other words, one of the major problems today is that, while some have a faith which touches their emotions, and others have a faith which tells what is right and wrong, few have a faith which touches their conduct. Renewal never comes until God's Word determines what we practice and not only what we profess.

Herein lies the challenge. For finally it is when faith fades into mere form and loses its power to guide people that a nation declines and falls.

15. Greatness and Gentleness

"God is strong enough to be gentle." This statement is the only thing I remember from an article I scanned recently. The words stay with me. When I reflect on them, several things grow in my thinking.

First, weakness of character makes persons demanding, exacting, and inconsiderate of others. Our attitudes toward others probably grow out of our own feelings of security or insecurity.

Some time ago a teacher tried to impress upon me that a certain student had a lot of self-confidence because he bragged about himself. The opposite was likely true. A braggart is one unsure of himself. It's the insecure youngster in school who threatens to beat others up. When you see a bully, you see one who is unsure of himself. When you see one making demands upon others, it is most likely a person who isn't sure of his own position.

A weak or insecure teacher or parent must threaten in an effort to get obedience. Therefore they yell, storm, and strike out at every infraction. Every infraction is a threat to one's security.

Insecure leaders, in the world or church, usually try to rule with an iron hand. They cannot afford to have their opinions and conclusions challenged. They develop a dogmatic disposition and delight in docile disciples. Such are afraid of free discussion or trusting the group in decisions because they fear the weakness of their own viewpoints. Or they quickly label other viewpoints as conservative or liberal in order to escape dealing with contrasting concerns.

On the other hand, one who is strong is gentle and gracious. This does not mean he has no firm beliefs. It does not mean he is spineless or wishy-washy. Persons who have spiritual strength and assurance and know what they believe, and why, can most easily stand differences of opinion and voices which challenge their own viewpoint. They can be gentle because they, like God, are strong in love and in the desire to help.

When love is weak, faith is weak. When faith is weak, love is weak. When it is hard to love another, faith is weak no matter how hard one may seek to defend the faith. When faith and love are weak, hard feelings and lack of trust develop easily. A critical spirit takes over. Weakness of faith leads to censuring others.

So it is the gentleness of God which enables us to become better persons. It is when we sense how strong God is that we see how gentle He is to us in all our sinfulness and helplessness. It is when we sense this great gentleness that we rise to new spiritual stature and strength. As the psalmist expressed it in some of his last words, "Thy gentleness hath made me great" (2 Samuel 22:36 and Psalm 18:35).

We should remind ourselves again and again that we really lead others only by moral and spiritual strength. The strong arm of outward control, rigid rules, authority derived from position does not lead. It holds sway only until people can get free from the control. Some have sought to demand leadership long after they have lost it because they tried to lead by the power of their position or some rule rather than by the strength of love and inner spiritual stature.

Another truth is bound into the statement, "God is strong enough to be gentle." When one is great, he is concerned about the little as well as the big things. The strength of God is just in that He is great enough to be concerned about the smallest things of life.

As a boy I was bothered many times by the thought that God was so great He could not possibly be concerned with me. One day I read a statement which said that God is not only concerned about the big things but He is so great He can be and is concerned about the smallest thing. He keeps account of the hair of my head. He notices every bump or brush burn I receive. As the psalmist said, I can go nowhere or think no thought except He is there and He knows. Now that's real greatness. It was only as I saw this truth that I saw God in His true greatness.

So the more we consider real strength, the more we see that real strength shows itself in caring about the smallest things and the most insignificant persons. Strength shows itself in its gentleness toward others. God in His strength rules over the universe. Yet He is gentle enough to be concerned with the smallest child. No wonder the Scripture says, "He will feed his flock like a shepherd, he will gather the lambs in his arms, he will carry them in his bosom, and gently lead those that are with young."

16. "Everybody's Doing It"

The "byword to hell" these days is "everybody's doing it." It's rather revealing and devastating when all too late many times, parents learn that all parents hear the same words they assumed they alone were hearing, "but everybody's doing it."

All along they thought they were the only ones in favor of not doing it. Now suddenly they realize that there were other parents who felt the same. What "everybody" was letting loose on because "everybody was doing it" turns out to be the thing "everybody" is against and "everybody" is afraid to stand against alone. The small slogan that pressures many parents into permissiveness is "but everybody's doing it."

This byword, "everybody's doing it," steps into and gains sanction even in the most sacred areas of life. "Everybody" lives an illicit sex life according to one report. "Everybody" practices marital unfaithfulness at some time or another, says a different report. "Everybody" dresses immodestly when summer comes. "Everybody" dances and drinks. "Everybody" is getting new furniture and finery. "Everybody" this and "everybody" that. The assumption back of it all is that if "everybody" does it, it puts on it a certain stamp of sacred sanction, an all right appearance and appraisal. Ever since the building of the tower of Babel man tries to make group action a substitute for God.

The fact is that Christians also become susceptible to such a slogan. "Everybody's doing it" takes precedence over God's will or even the search for what God's will is. Suddenly, because other Christians or church members are doing it, then it must be right. Adolescent-like, the Christian does not dare to be different.

But "everybody" isn't doing it! Neither is every Christian doing it. Look a little further and you find it isn't true at all. Many have not bowed the knee to Baal. The "everybody's doing it" philosophy is a device of the devil to deceive. It's the byword to hell.

In fact, the Christian knows that when he says, "Everybody's doing it," it is likely not the thing for him to do at all. This may be the very warning light telling him to beware. No, he does not take the attitude that the Christian deliberately does everything contrary to what others do without real reason. It means, however, that he is firmly persuaded and called to realize that the current of society is not and never was Christian.

Paul saw the deadly danger of this philosophy. He cries to the Christians at Rome: "You in Rome must stand against the philosophy which says, 'When in Rome do as the Romans do.' Don't be squeezed into the world's mold. You must stand against it all. You must emerge in purity from all this impurity. You must live righteously in the midst of unrighteousness. Dare to be different even in Rome. You do not live by herd instinct. You must live in defiance of all the worldly attitudes of this ungodly age. Don't be squeezed into its mold of thought and practice."

When regimentation seems to be the character of our age, we are required to take our stand under God. Next time you are tempted to say, "Everybody's doing it," stop long enough to think. Stop long enough to ask a few questions. Is it right? What is God's will? Be courageous enough to stand for Christian conviction.

Somehow I'm made to feel that God and our needy world are waiting for those who live by a greater guide for actions than "everybody's doing it."

17. A Sense of Well-Being

Some claim there is a great difference in family needs which allows some to give more to the Lord's work and limits others. Such say that some have a greater need for things or luxuries of life in order to feel a sense of well-being or fulfillment. Other families seem happy with much less.

I'm not at all sure. Such reasoning can so easily become an excuse for selfish indulgence. It allows a logic to keep in the latest styles, to purchase exquisite furniture, or to live a luxurious life in general. And because of what is excused as personal needs for our own well-being, the Lord's work suffers.

If it is true that things are what give us a sense of well-being, what happens when all things are taken away? This has happened to Christians in years past. Who dare say it will not happen again? There is nothing as uncertain and insecure as things. Will we have them tomorrow? No one knows. If not, does the loss of things mean the loss of well-being? Or do we, as Christians, really believe that in every condition in which we find ourselves we can be content because we know and have Christ? Can we rejoice in everything? This was the Apostle Paul's view.

When Dwight L. Moody lost all of his earthly possessions in the great Chicago fire, someone said to him, "Mr. Moody, I suppose you lost everything." "Oh, no," said Moody, "I still have Christ."

Following Christ really means a readiness to drop all things at any moment in order to follow Him more completely. To be Christ's disciple means that nothing will be allowed to come between Christ and us. In fact, Christ seems to say that we dare not let our sense of well-being be tied to things in themselves. He came to save us from the tyranny of things. He tells us in Matthew 7:32 that it is characteristic of the heathen to make well-being hinge on things. In Luke 12:20 Christ calls the person a fool who lays up things for himself and is not rich toward God.

As long as we seek our well-being or satisfaction in things, the thirst for things and a sense of satisfaction will never be fulfilled. Check, if you will, with those who seem to have everything. I've known enough of such to know that they have everything but a sense of well-being.

Further, there is a clear sense in which, when we hint that our sense of well-being is dependent upon things, we are really saying that we are more worthy than others who do not have things.

Do we believe we have a right or Christian privilege to withhold our giving or to live on a higher standard than others merely because we live in a land of abundance? Because we have the means to buy things we assume we are more worthy. Or, do we, because we live in a land of affluence, have a greater responsibility to give a higher percentage of our income than where affluence is not known?

Stewardship is primarily an attitude of commitment. It is a commitment which flows from a love response. We commit ourselves to what or whom we love. And we are committed to so much today.

72

To what or to whom do we commit ourselves? We choose what we want to commit ourselves to. It is not a question as to whether we have commitments. We commit ourselves to building or paying off a home, a new car, attending the activities and programs of the neighborhood, and keeping up with the Joneses.

So it seems it is not so much a matter of different needs which persons have as different commitments which determine what is given to the Lord's work. Where our money goes is determined by what or whom we love, for commitment flows from a love response.

"Do not lay up for yourselves treasures on earth, where moth and rust consume and where thieves break in and steal, but lay up for yourselves treasures in heaven, where neither moth nor rust consumes and where thieves do not break in and steal. For where your treasure is, there will your heart be also" (Matthew 6:19-21). And Jesus said, "Take heed, and beware of all covetousness; for a man's life does not consist in the abundance of his possessions" (Luke 12:15). "For the love of money is the root of all evils; it is through this craving that some have wandered away from the faith and pierced their hearts with many pangs" (1 Timothy 6:10).

18. Searching for Substitutes

We live in a day of substitutes. Many are available at much less cost than the real thing. Yet they appear to be the real thing. They seem to do the same job. And, in fact, many substitutes may do as well as the real item.

Some things have no substitutes. What is often offered looks like the real thing. If tried, it may seem for a while to do the same job. Yet when put to the test, we see it as only a substitute.

Take prayer. There is no substitute for prayer. Either you practice daily prayer or you are a pauper in spiritual power. It doesn't matter how many meetings you attend. You might give scores of speeches. But unless you spend some time face to face with God each day, you are not living a vital dynamic life. We need regular times for prayer. We need a prayer list of concerns. There is no substitute for prayer.

There is no substitute for the study of the Word. The Scripture must be lovingly digested for spiritual growth. Only on this foundation can one build a strong superstructure of spiritual service. Then one is equipped to continue faithful to Christ in the current of the world.

You can't substitute personal search of the Word by listening to a hundred sermons, reading all the theology of modern-day theologians, or becoming acquainted with many books about the Bible. There is no substitite for personal study.

Or take the matter of witnessing. Perhaps there is no area where so many substitutes are sought as in witnessing. We invite people to church; we tell them to be good in many ways; we plan for all kinds of programs for fellowship without sharing Christ Himself. Witnessing is introducing others to a person. It is not only living a godly life. It is telling that which you have seen and heard. There is no substitute for this. Unless one is a witness for Christ he is more a hazard than a help.

Now all this is true also in the life of the church. The church has as much power as her persistent prayer life. The church is as strong as her study of the Word. The impact on the world is in proportion to the willingness to witness. We cannot seek to substitute something else for these and still have a strong spiritual church.

Why do we try to substitute in spiritual things? Because we are not willing to do what it takes for the real thing. It's hard to pray, study the Word, and be a faithful witness. It's much easier and simpler to substitute something else. We think there are shortcuts to spiritual maturity, spiritual renewal, and soul saving. So we devise parties, contests, specials, and loads of activities thinking that they just have to work.

But somehow they don't. Why? We cannot feed people's spiritual hunger with anything but spiritual food. There is no other place to receive power except from God. The way of witnessing is still the same: "Ye shall be witnesses unto me."

There are times and places for parties, contests, specials, and other good activities. Who has not enjoyed these! They can be the means of strengthening us spiritually. But facing it honestly, few are brought to the gates of salvation by these. We dare never think that when we have done these, we have done our duty. Souls are still won today by prayer, the Word, and personal witness. There really are no substitutes.

19. What's Right About the Church

"Christ also loved the church, and gave himself for it" (Ephesians 5:25).

The sermon title which I saw in a church bulletin some time ago was, "What's Right About the Church?" It struck me. I wished I could have heard the sermon. I do not know at all what was said. But it started me thinking, and I've come to see afresh that we do not think about this truth enough.

There is too much hand wringing over the church. The church is blamed for many evils. People are saying, "What's wrong with the church? What is it doing to relieve injustice, inequality, and wrong? It isn't relevant."

We even hear folks talk of the post-Christian era. But there never was a Christian era.

The Bible says true Christians will be a misunderstood nucleus, a dedicated, despised, and dwindling minority. It has always been true.

But what's right about the church? The church is the only body in the world calling men to God through Christ. No other body is charged with this responsibility. It alone is the "foundation and pillar of truth." If the church does not lay the foundation of truth and uphold truth, none other will. The church alone proclaims peace and pardon to perishing people. It alone has man's most needed message: "Come again into close companionship with God through Christ."

The church alone gives guidance and help, warning and comfort from the cradle to the grave. It places value on the smallest and weakest. It guides the strongest and greatest. It cares for those being born and for those dying. All of life between does not escape its concern. The baby, the youth, the home, the old are its concern. Even for life beyond, the church gives a glorious hope. One wrote, "I have just returned from my mother's funeral, and one thought keeps ringing in my heart: 'Thank God for the church.' In times of grief and trial the church has meant so much to me!"

Who else holds the sick and suffering up

before God in prayer? The church gives encouragement when the world scorns. It gives a message of hope when the world gives despair.

The church leads in compassion for the world. The church is a blessing everywhere it goes in purity and power. Lives are uplifted, made holy and loving. Who but the church really cares for the sinner?

Paul says in Colossians 1:4-6: Wherever the message of the church goes it creates faith in Jesus Christ, love for all the saints, a hope of heaven, and bears the same kind of fruit — the fruit of love, joy, peace, kindness, gentleness, goodness, faith. No matter the climate or country, the need or nationality, the condition or color, this is true.

The church is the only forgiving community on the earth. It alone has the message of forgiveness, and it alone knows the method and meaning of forgiveness.

Hospitals, schools, orphanages, homes for the aged are the result of the church's compassion. Follow the church from land to land, and these follow it as well. Let critics and hypocrites cry and harp against and about the church. No infidel, critic, or hypocrite ever began such work, and the church's critics have led the world backward and not forward.

The church sets the moral tone of the community and is by its life the conscience of God in society. P. T. Barnum, the prominent circus man, once said, "Show me a place where there are not any churches, and I will show you a place where old hats are stuffed in the windows, where gates have no hinges, where women are slipshod, and where maps of the devil's wild land are printed on men's shirt bosoms with tobacco juice."

Teddy Roosevelt told how that in the early settling of America, wherever a community started without the church, it started from that point on the road to heathendom, destruction, and disappearance.

Never forget, the church begins and ends with God. It is not human. It is divine. It was declared dead many times, yet lives. It stands the test of time. "The gates of hell shall not prevail against it." The power and presence of Christ, Lord of the church, perpetuates the church. Let Pharaohs, Herods, Stalins come and go to do what they will, the church is the anvil that still breaks many a hammer. It continues to tower over the wrecks of time. And when communism and every other ism dies, the church will still be around for its funeral.

"Oh, where are kings and empires now
  Of old that went and came?
But, Lord, Thy church is praying yet,
  A thousand years the same."

It is possible to destroy the church building, but not Christ's body — the church. One Saturday night during World War II, London was bombed. A neighborhood church building was completely destroyed. The next morning the people gathered in a semicircle amid the ruins and sang "The church's one Foundation is Jesus Christ her Lord."

When the church meets hardship, persecution, and peril instead of peace and prosperity, it does not mean failure. It may mean merely that the church, strong and godly, is drawing the power of evil and opposition.

Probably the finest name ever given to the church, outside the Bible, is Bunyan's "Palace Beautiful." Yet the churches of Bunyan's day were little better than barns. But seated there Bunyan could look above the crude and cramping benches, the dingy and rough rafters, and the leaking roofs to see the true church of Jesus Christ in its beauty, glory, grandeur, and grace. He saw the church for whom Christ died, the church deserving the dedication of our lives — even unto death.

What's right about the church? Enough that no one need drag his feet or despair. Enough that no believer should lose heart. Enough that every Christian should unhesitatingly throw himself into the most alive and lasting work in the world — the work of the church.

20. Selective Obedience

In a recent meeting with leaders from many different denominations I was impressed with how all of us seem to practice selective obedience. Regardless of what group we belong to we tend to take from the Scriptures those things we choose to stress and obey. We act as though some commands of God are optional.

For instance, have we practiced selective obedience in such areas as loving and praying for our enemies, seeking things which make for peace and being instruments of reconciliation, in giving a proper portion of our income, in being filled with the Spirit, in giving to the needy, in confessing our faults one to another and praying one for another?

What happens when we practice selective obedience?

First, we pick those things which we feel we are doing best or which can be done the easiest. This is why externals of one kind or another so easily become a distinction of one group or another. Then we laud our heritage as though we were completely faithful descendants.

To pretend to practice anything perfectly leads to Pharisaism, the spirit that denounces all who do not practice as we understand it. A Pharisaical spirit can so easily catch us regardless of who we are. Some who claim freedom from tradition or certain teaching may be as Pharisaical as those who are committed to what they consider essential.

After denunciation comes de-Christianization. Those who do not or will not do or see what we do or see cannot possibly be Christian. Some who will fight for their position on non-resistance and condemn others for a different stance become very selective in their obedience to Scripture which speaks of responsibilities for peacemaking and love among brethren.

The glorious thing, if we really want to see it, is that God so made us and operates in us by His Spirit that we can help each other to a fuller and fuller understanding of and obedience to His will. The very fact that I have shared with others what I consider to be a neglected truth and that others share with me the truth in love means that both are blessed and helped to fuller obedience.

All of us know how easy it is to have blind spots. This means we need each other. I doubt whether anyone can grow in grace and in the knowledge of Jesus Christ without fellow Christians who are willing to be used of God in sharing their insight into Scripture. This is the means of building up each other into mature persons compacted by that which every part supplies.

21. Domesticated Bible

That's what the speaker called it — a "domesticated Bible." A "domesticated Bible" is one which is tamed so that it can be handled. It doesn't control us. We control it. We read from it and in it just what we want to in order to confirm an old stand, prove the right of a present wish, or to conform another in what he should or should not do or believe.

A "domesticated Bible" is one to which we may go for proof texts rather than the place we go to find God speaking to us "now." We may tame the Bible until somehow it doesn't dare change our lives or standards. The Bible is so tamed at times it just will not jump the fences of our present faith or pull the leash by which we hold it in control.

A "domesticated Bible" allows us to walk our own way and seems to support us by following and sanctioning our desires. We might find it supporting and sanctioning segregation, war, division of brethren, riches, or certain forms or practices. It is domesticated to the point that it will listen to us and obey us in changing every personal threat or feeling when we say "mind."

A "domesticated Bible" is one which just isn't allowed to bark loud against certain sins. It may make much noise at the sins which are safe (those of which we are not guilty), but remain quiet about our own. It may make much against war but it is not allowed to speak as strongly against ill will and divisions. The leash may be lengthened so that it will leap out against the evils of drink but be tamed never to notice the pressing evils of the thief who robs God of His tithes and offerings. It may do a fine job of protecting the house from strangers and also of keeping quiet and sleeping in its box when it should speak to confrontation with our communities.

The Bible may be so domesticated that we may wonder if it is alive at all. It comes to know its place. We put it there and it doesn't bother to show itself or come to one's attention regardless of what happens.

Even then, if we take the trouble to touch it and take it seriously, it is found to be alive. If we go so far as to really desire that it jump the fences of our present faith to an enlarging vision and trust in what God says and does, it will not fail. If we allow the controls to be taken from our hands and let the Word lead us, we will find it worthy of our trust. If we will go far enough to let the Word become so active that it should demand radical change, regardless of what, we will find it will not make unfair demands.

Believing the Bible to be God's Word means more than being able to recite, "All scripture is given by inspiration of God," or similar phrases as important as these are. It means that we allow that Word to speak to us and let it make its claim on us in absolute surrender and obedience. It means we will not make it suit our desires but rather let it become our directive in all of life.

22. Cult of Comfort

The cult of comfort is popular. It minimizes the aspect of the Christian gospel represented by the cross and stresses the usefulness of Christ and religion as a means of making people happy. God becomes a sort of glorified Santa Claus to get what we want. He becomes a means for easy living, winning friends, and influencing people.

The cult of comfort follows the line that "if an unhappy thought enters your mind, immediately stop it, toss it out by substituting immediately a happy thought." Now the trick of it all is that there is some truth to this. It appears at first so lovely and noble we are inclined to say, "How fine! It sounds Christian." But it isn't!

This is not what Paul is speaking about in Philippians 4:8: — "Whatsoever things are true, whatsoever things are honest, whatsoever things are just, whatsoever things are pure, whatsoever things are lovely, whatsoever things are of good report; if there be any virtue, and if there be any praise, think on these things."

Look at Jesus in Gethsemane. He steadfastly set His face to Jerusalem. His thoughts were on suffering and dying. The cross was ahead. He knew it. Nor did He try to push this, the will of God, from His mind because it was an unpleasant thought to His flesh. He spoke of it to His disciples and told them the way of the cross was the way of every disciple. "If any man will come after me, let him deny himself, and take up his cross, and follow me."

The cult of comfort does not like self-denial. It loves self-indulgence, modern conveniences, and a life acceptable to the world first of all. The cross is out. It is recognized only as a golden polished piece hanging on the wall or around the neck. To really follow Christ through a death experience to self, this thought cannot be endured. Replace such thoughts with fine words about "everybody smile and be happy," and "let's be merry because it's the only way to really live."

The truth is that such philosophy has led to a shocking thing today. In the midst of great evil and peril in our world, many remain complacently indifferent. We just don't want to think of the facts of our times. It requires too much. It is too unpleasant.

One of the reasons Jesus is remembered is that He said, "Take up your cross and follow me." He would have been forgotten years ago had He merely said, "Everybody smile and be happy."

Today Jesus still calls: "Deny yourself to follow the Father's will; take the cross which always results from such denial and follow me through a resurrection experience to a new life for God."

23. Past, Present, Future

It is characteristic of man to delight in the past, to disbelieve the present, and to dread the future. He speaks of the "good old days" which cannot be relived. His disbelief in the present makes today meaningless and miserable. His dread of the future makes every day dreary and full of drudgery.

In a limited sense it is good to think of the past. Looking at the past properly can make it a stepping-stone to the future. To notice past mistakes ought to help us to future victories. But to think only on lost opportunities, to rehash forgiven sins, or to describe the past as being all good and glorious at the expense of the present is shameful.

Forgetting those things which are behind,

we must press on. To draw comparisons with the past to the detriment of today leads to folding our arms and bowing down as worshipers of the past. We know those who talk about what they used to do.

One beyond middle age glories in telling what he used to give to the church. Yet now he is in good health, his family is grown, and he has financial ability to give more than in the years past. He is sitting today in a seat of self-satisfaction. When we stop living in the present, we start reliving the past.

The "good old days" — when were they? It's hard to tell. A slab, more than three thousand years old, was dug up in Babylonia. It read, "Alas, alas, times are not now what they used to be."

Too often we spend hours thinking and worrying over the past. But we don't plow a furrow by looking over our shoulders. Looking back we become pillars of salt.

Then there are those who disbelieve the present. Everything is going to the dogs. The nation, the church, the home, and the young people are completely corrupted. Someone suggested that things have been going to the dogs for so long that it is a wonder the dogs haven't taken over.

94

Without a doubt there is much to depress and sadden one. Society seems to be swinging back to savagery rather than away from it. But God is not dead! Said J. D. Jones, "Our doubts and despairs arise from the fact that we have made Him [God] altogether like ourselves."

We must constantly guard against the church's condition corresponding to the condition of the age. The devil desires few things as much as a down-in-the-mouth Christian. He desires to drive us to doubt and discouragement — doubt as to the ability of the great God we serve and discouragement as to the triumph of the cause of Christ through every age and condition.

Put it down, the person who is always bemoaning our ineffectiveness, our lack of power, and our lack of confidence isn't doing much for God, the church, or the world. Pessimism is a part of the apostasy of the latter days. It says Christ is not on the throne; everything depends on man; God is too slow!

This does not mean we put on rose-colored glasses. There is a superabounding sin, disobedience, worldliness, coldness, and lethargy. We need to notice these facts until they put our hearts on fire and push us to our knees in prayer. Until this happens we aren't really concerned anyway. Along with this realization and action we must realize that the Christian has the remedy in the gospel. God is on the throne. Christ is still mighty to save. It is because we lost sight of God that we are so soon on edge.

We must have a proper perspective of the present. We are called to serve this generation according to the will of God. We cannot live in any other time.

Then, too, we can disbelieve and deplore the present so that life loses its luster and meaning. A Christian is one who sees that not only was the past holy because God was there, but also the present is holy because God is here.

If we are going to be a blessing to our generation, we had better begin immediately. If we are ever going to serve, we dare not wait. God deals with us in the language of now. What moves God to give us tomorrow if we don't use today?

How about the future? Most people dread it, fear it, or endeavor to ignore it. All these are wrong. Unless we have hope for the future, the present becomes meaningless.

What about tomorrow? There are two ways of facing it. One is the way of anxiety and despair and pessimism. Ann Landers has written: "No one puts it in so many words, but there is in our viewpoint today a suggestion that we may as well live it up fast because tomorrow may never come. And among too many teenagers, living it up fast is expressed in accelerated dating, early smoking and drinking, sexual experience, premature marriage, and premature divorce." Doesn't this describe our age?

The other alternative is to take the way of the Creator who called us not to death but to life. He has spoken. His words are hope and life. This old world cannot be saved from its downward course and doom except by Jesus Christ. Only as we take His word of love and forgiveness and trust Him can we be prepared for the future. When this happens, fear of the future is driven from our hearts. We answer with the Apostle Paul: "For I am persuaded, that neither death, nor life, nor angels, nor principalities, nor powers, nor things present, nor things to come, nor height, nor depth, nor any other creature, shall be able to separate us from the love of God, which is in Christ Jesus our Lord" (Romans 8:38, 39).

24. They Didn't Fly

Soren Kierkegaard, the Danish philosopher, one time told a parable which went something like this:

A flock of geese lived together in a barnyard. Once a week they gathered in one corner of the yard. One of the most eloquent speakers mounted the fence to speak about the wonders and grandeur of geese. The speaker spoke of the exploits of their ancestors.

Their forefathers, the preacher goose declared, explored the trackless wastes of the sky with powerful wings. In goodness the Creator gave geese wondrous wings to fly and planted within them the urge to migrate.

Not only did the geese listen attentively each week but they nodded their heads in solemn approval. When the preaching goose was done, those who listened complimented him prettily on his learning and eloquence.

Now this happened every week. One thing did not happen, however. They never did fly. They went back to their waiting dinner, for the corn was good and barnyard secure.

❖   ❖   ❖

Perhaps the meaning of the parable is so plain it is useless to pursue it further. Then again it might be good to note several applications.

Just as wings which are not used finally will not bear the weight of a bird in flight, so light ignored turns to darkness and belief which does not determine behavior becomes blind and dead. The Christian today is not dying from lack of information. He is weak because the good corn and the security of the barnyard have his first love. The divine urge to mission is one to which we listen attentively and nod our heads in solemn approval.

Surely the test of the Christian is at the point of how he responds to the call of Christ to suffering and death. How much will he dare for Christ? Yes, there is danger in venturing beyond our own yard. The only alternative is to grow fat and lazy. Here is real danger.

At this moment it is inward apathy and not outside opposition which threatens Christians — at least in America. Love of ease and a consuming passion for passing things lock our lips and keep our wings clipped or folded. It is true that most of us gather once a week to hear of our Creator's goodness and our possibilities in Christ. The real issue is whether we will return to living the same as before and love the security of the present more than doing Christ's will.

Thomas a Kempis wrote, "All desire to rejoice with Him; few are willing to undergo anything for His sake. Many follow Jesus that they may eat of His loaves, but few that they might drink of the cup of His passion. Many are astonished at His miracles; few follow after the shame of His cross."

How often we avoid Christ's call because of the cross; yet it is first the cross, then the crown. George Failing writes, "The Calvary thread is missing from the 'Christian' skein of life. We can see no purpose in suffering or poverty or death. Superficially we believe that God purposes for each of us only health, wealth, honor, first-class citizenship! But the true measure of life's worth is the ability to worthily suffer and die. Good health and good housing are not salvation; they may be only narcotics that help poor souls to exist before they die."

How often we merely love to speak of the exploits of the apostles or our own ancestors. We extol those who climbed the steep ascent through blood and toil and pain. But who follows in their train? Who demonstrates equal devotion? Who walks the path of the same obedience?

The answer to our need today lies not in making the dark night hideous with lamentations. The answer is not to stand aloof from our world or to yield in spineless conformity to our society. Again let it be said that the challenge in the next decade or century will be in what we will dare for Christ. Will we obey Christ regardless of the cost? Will we be disciples till death? "And they overcame him by the blood of the Lamb, and by the word of their testimony; and they loved not their lives unto the death" (Revelation 12:11).

25. We're Known
for Humility

The other day I heard my four-year-old speaking to her baby sister while they played on the lawn. She spoke concerning family devotions. "Come, Rosie," she said. "We are going to have our demotions."

Many times as believers, we need to bow before our living Lord to see afresh our own unworthiness and His exceeding grace. Our own imaginations and high personal desires must be cast down so that God may be glorified through us.

Humility is a grace which you have already lost when you think you have it. I read of a man who wrote a book entitled *Humility and How I Attained It*. Perhaps you heard of the preacher who said he had a wonderful sermon on humility and he was just waiting for a large enough audience to preach it.

Then there is the statement attributed to a Carthusian monk. "The Dominicans," he said, "are famous for their learning, and the Franciscans for their piety, but when it comes to humility, we're tops."

Love is spoken of as an unselfish grace. Patience is an unwearing grace. Humility is an unconscious grace. We might counterfeit love, faith, or peace, but true humility cannot be counterfeited since it is best seen in lowly service.

True humility always causes one to feel he gets more favor than he deserves. The humble person is anxious that God gets the glory. The proud person desires at least some glory for himself. The humble person is not easily hurt. The proud takes offense quickly.

A proud person is conscious primarily of what he is doing and exaggerates this far beyond its proper proportions. This is pictured humorously by Aesop who tells of a fly sitting upon an axletree of a chariot wheel. The fly exclaimed, "What a dust do I raise!"

Humility does not come from asceticism, a certain robe, or pious speech. It is not realized by seclusion, starving oneself by fasting, or sleeping on boards. These may and usually do pamper pride.

True humility is an unconscious grace which results from a proper estimate of our own unworthiness of God's exceeding great grace.

A father and his little boy walked down a street in Chicago past the place where a skyscraper was being constructed. Glancing up they saw the men at work on a high story of the building.

"Father," said the little boy, "what are those little boys doing up there?"

"Those are not little boys; those are grown men, Son."

"But why do they look so small?"

"Because they are so high," his father answered.

After a short pause the lad asked, "Then, Father, when they get to heaven, there won't be anything left of them, will there?"

It is true. The nearer we come to Christ, the less others see of us and the more they see of Christ.

26. Prosperity Perils

We are wooed and won today by treasure, pleasure, and leisure. We work for these, live for these, and die for these. There are few things we are tempted with as much as things, thrills, and time we haven't learned how to use wisely.

It's hard to hear God in times of prosperity. "In prosperity the destroyer shall come" (Job 15:21). We become so self-sufficient and supposedly satisfied. Of old God said, "I spoke to you in your prosperity, but you said, 'I will not listen'" (Jeremiah 22:21). The vision and voice of God are blurred, sometimes entirely banished, when so much as a small coin is held too close to the eyes or let fall on the pavement of a business venture.

We live today in the lap of luxury. Kings of the past did not know anything comparable to the present life of the average American citizen. We are being crushed by our comforts and conveniences. Most of us face the peril of plenty rather than the peril of poverty. No nation has withstood prosperity in the past. It is a perilous position, for while thousands stand through poverty, few stand through prosperity.

Perhaps the place we err the most in not heeding the warning of Christ is in thinking that we are not blessed. We apply Christ's warnings regarding money to the financial tycoon or the tightfisted miser. Worse yet, we have such deep desires for so many more things that we fool ourselves into thinking we have little.

What was it that brought such awful judgment on Sodom? Are you inclined to say immorality first? But no, listen, "Behold, this was the iniquity of thy sister Sodom, pride, fulness of bread, and abundance of idleness was in her and in her daughters, neither did she strengthen the hand of the poor and needy" (Ezekiel 16:49).

Politicians, nearly any preacher or person, can become famous today by simply saying,

106

We are the greatest people in the world (pride); we must raise our own standard of living (fullness of bread); we must shorten our working hours (idleness); we must take care of ourselves and our surpluses (ignoring the world's poor and needy). And people love it.

Let him who thinks he deserves not God's fire and brimstone because he is moral and manages his business well look carefully at the perils of prosperity: pride, plenty to eat, long vacations, and a heart which does not ache and act for the poor and needy. For "In prosperity the destroyer shall come."

This is a time of great prosperity and peril — prosperity to the few who happen to be born where barns are full and stockpiles darken the sun — peril to all, especially to us who have so much.

It is also time to humble ourselves in recognition of God's goodness to us. It is time to eat our food as those who know also how to fast and work as those who know the night is near. It is time, in our land of abundance and affluence, that we pause long enough to hear the cry of anguished mothers watching their little ones slowly dying for lack of food and catch sight of those who lack homes and live in rags.

It is time we do not simply pray, "Bless those who have not as we do," but rather reach deep into our God-given resources and respond with a stewardship which strengthens the hand of the poor and needy, asking nothing in return. Only then will we escape the perils of prosperity and the destruction that may lie ahead.

27. Youth–What's the Problem?

Interesting insight is gained by taking time to read the literature of the past and compare it with what we produce today. What is being discussed today differs so little from descriptions written centuries ago.

One of the most familiar statements about youth was said by Socrates around 400 B.C. "Our youth love luxury. They have bad manners, contempt for authority, disrespect for older people. Children nowadays are tyrants. They no longer rise when their elders enter the room. They contradict their parents, chatter before company, gobble their food, and tyrannize their teachers."

In A.D. 383 the great Augustine describes why he quit as a college professor at

Carthage. "The students are disgracefully out of control. They come breaking into class in the most unmannerly way, and behaving almost like madmen, disturb the order which the master has established for the good of his pupils. They commit a number of disorderly acts which show an incredible stupidity and which ought to be punished by law. However, custom protects them" (Augustine, *Confessions*, Book V, Chapter VIII).

We are always inclined to feel the past was about perfect. Just today again someone spoke of the good old days. You know the days when all was religious and righteous. To pine for the past really is to live in "the good old daze." Previous centuries had both good and bad. Since people are so similar by nature, not much new in human behavior has developed since Eden.

One philosopher described youth of every age when he wrote, "Youth is usually right in what it opposes and usually wrong in what it proposes."

Those who know what youth are saying today find them right in what they oppose. They may have limited their targets. They may not be sensitive in all areas. Who is? Yet they clearly oppose sham, war, hypocrisy, bad ethics, and cruel injustices. H. L. Mencken many years ago wrote: "Youth, though it may lack knowledge, is certainly not devoid of intelligence; it sees through shams with sharp and terrible eyes."

We may take issue because of the way youth oppose the wrong, but it is good for older persons to realize that it has always been the character of youth to protest. As Benjamin Disraeli told the House of Commons in 1859, "Youth is somewhat reckless in assertion, and when one is juvenile and curly one takes pride in sarcasm."

Francis Bacon adds, "Young men are fitter to invent than to judge, fitter for execution than for counsel, and fitter for new projects than for settled business."

So it is not quite fair, no matter how fine it sounds, to blame youth today for our problems, or for protesting without providing answers. We should hardly expect youth to provide answers. Youth has not had the experience to provide good answers. That's the work for the older generation. It's enough if the youth can remind us of the things we should oppose. The job of youth, in each generation, seems to be to prick the conscience of its time, in whatever way it can, from poetry to more active protest, and press for decisions which, without youth prodding, would not be made.

After all, what would our world be like if it were not for youth who keep us from going to sleep in our sins? Age seems to despair of the agony of dealing with the devil. Age comes to accept his antics and although its preaching remains correct its preformance has a tendency to become corrupt.

Age, although it speaks against sin, tends to accept it. As Amy Lowell wrote, "Youth condemns; maturity condones."

In *Near to the Heart of God* Cleland B. Afee wrote, "The universe is not altogether as God meant it to be. We are here partly to change it. One of His mercies is that as men grow older and used to things, He takes them away and puts the universe in the hands of young, fresh men."

Here's where youth comes with all its antagonism to sham and injustice and cuts open the conscience and lays bare the inadequacy of us all. So even today's "rebellion of youth" may show us more about the condition of our own inner soul than we are willing to admit. In a real sense each generation has the youth it deserves. To admit we are inadequate, that we have failed, that we are sinners is like skinning ourselves alive. But that's what repentance is. Were it not for a new generation of youth to denounce the sin it sees, in one or two generations we'd all be in hell.

28. Listen, You!

President Nixon made a very important point when, in his inaugural address, he said, "We cannot learn from one another until we stop shouting at one another — until we speak quietly enough so that our words can be heard as well as our voices."

Someone said, "There is no such thing as an unpopular listener."

The above remarks say a good bit about our gaps today. We are all too verbose. We can talk without thinking. But one cannot really listen without some thought. Strange as it may sound, good communication begins with listening, not with speaking.

Now look at one of the gaps we are reminded of constantly. It's the generation gap. The reason it is so big a gap is that neither side is doing much listening. Both sides are loud enough. Youth today are yelling. Youth are protesting and screaming. Even the music of today is so loud that few can think or talk, or for that matter, understand the words of the song. We hear but we don't listen.

On the other hand, adults aren't doing much listening either. Many parents have become pretty unpopular because they present all the answers before the questions are asked. Remember, "There is no such thing as an unpopular listener."

As adults we must learn to listen. We aren't listening until we actually hear what our youth are saying so clearly that we can say their words back again to their own satisfaction. Because we have authority we feel we should do the speaking. So we never get a chance to communicate because we will not listen first. Until one listens, his authority is not respected. Until one listens, he will largely be ignored.

One big way then to close the gap of our age is to listen. "We cannot learn from one another until we stop shouting at one another."

I found real encouragement to listen more in the book, *Life Together*, by Dietrich Bonhoeffer. "The first service," he said, "that one owes to others in the fellowship consists in listening to them. Just as love to God begins with listening to His Word, so the beginning of love for the brethren is learning to listen to them.

"Many people are looking for an ear that will listen. They do not find it among Christians, because these Christians are talking when they should be listening. But he who can no longer listen to his brother will soon be no longer listening to God either; he will be doing nothing but prattle in the presence of God. This is the beginning of the death of the spiritual life."

Christians ought to be the best listeners. Yet Christians are the ones accused very often of giving an answer before they hear the question.

Many times I've been surprised at the few words we have from Jesus. He was always surrounded by people and I suppose people were much like people today — looking for someone who would listen and ignoring the ones who didn't. I believe Jesus understood what was in man not only because He was divine but also because He listened intently. He heard the heart cry, the yearnings, and the need.

Christ's longest recorded sermon can be read

in fifteen minutes and some think that is a combination of several sermons. Be that as it may, let us confess we have a lot to learn in really listening to others. It may well be that the big reason our message is sometimes so superficial is that we see only the surface instead of really listening to what others are saying. Is it true that the beginning of our love to others is in learning to listen to them?

29. To Be Continued

On his seventy-fifth birthday, Victor Hugo wrote: "When I go down to the grave, I can say, like many others, 'I have finished my day's work.' But I cannot say, 'I have finished my life.' My day's work will begin again the next morning. The tomb is not a blind alley; it is a thoroughfare. It closes on the twilight. It opens on the dawn."

Only Christianity can claim an empty tomb. Christ's resurrection and promise of life prove that death will not have the final victory. If our hopes were limited to this life only, we should be pitied. But now Christ is raised from the dead and provides the proof that we too shall live.

Many months ago the gardener took brown,

dead-looking bulbs and buried them in the soil. Had the bulbs thinking ability, they might have said, "This is the end." Really it was only the beginning. Today the lilies' beauty bears testimony that it was only a beginning. Their floral fragrance tells us that not only is resurrection life real but the other side of death shall display a loveliness and triumph not known on this side. As a brown bulb in the black earth towers in triumph over the dark marsh, so in Christ's resurrection we see afresh that the blatant and clamorous forces of life are not final and that God's eternal message of beginning again, in Christ, means the triumph of life over death.

What nature every spring so clearly symbolizes, we have finalized for us in the words of Christ Himself: "I am the resurrection and the life; he who believes in me, though he die, yet shall he live, and whoever lives and believes in me shall never die" (John 11:25, 26). Again He says, "I am he that liveth, and was dead; and, behold, I am alive for evermore" (Revelation 1:18).

Halford E. Luccock tells the story of his little daughter, who went for the first time into the country to spend some time with her grandmother. Early one beautiful morning she looked out of her bedroom window and was thrilled to catch the vision of her first real sunrise. "O Grandma," she cried. "Wake up; the world is beginning!"

To the sensitive little girl the miracle of sunrise was much more than the beginning of a new day; it was like the dawning of a fresh new world. So to the sensitive soul Easter speaks not only of the resurrection of Christ but of the dawning of a new day for every person who believes in Christ. The resurrection is the beginning of new life. Without the mystery of the cross and the majesty of the resurrection, there would be no gospel to preach to sinful and dying men. But "life and immortality are brought to light through the gospel."

Probably the two things which concern man most are these: the meaning of life here and the possibilities of life hereafter — or life and immortality. These are understood only through the gospel. "Do people die with you? Have you no charm against death?" These sad questions of the natives gathered around David Livingstone in deep Africa many years ago voice the query of every heart.

J. R. Green in *A Short History of the English People* tells of the coming of Christianity to Northumbria. The wise men of Northumbria gathered to discuss and weigh the reasons for and against the new faith that Paulinus, follower of Augustine, brought to England. The appeal lay in the light it cast on the origin of man's life and its final destiny.

During the discussion, an aged alderman arose and said: "So seems the life of man, O King . . . as a sparrow's flight through the hall where you are sitting at meat in wintertide, with the warm fire lighted on the hearth, but the icy rainstorm without. The sparrow flies in at one door and tarries for a moment in the light and heat of the hearth-fire, and then flying forth from the other door vanishes into the wintry darkness from whence it came. So tarries for a moment the life of man in our sight, but what is before it, and after it, we know not. If this new teaching tells us aught certainty of these things, let us follow it."

The philosophies of man cannot reason the purpose of life here. They cannot give life meaning. Nor can man's philosophies reason that the soul must be immortal. T. de Witt Talmage wrote: "Philosophic speculation has gone through heaven, and told us there is no

121

gold there; through hell, and told us there is no fire there; and through the grave, and told us there is no resurrection, and has left hanging over all the future one great, thick London fog." At best, human reason can only hope. But Jesus can say, "Whosoever liveth and believeth on me shall never die."

Resurrection faith says that in the resurrection of Jesus is provided the source of our faith in life and death. It says death is not the end but the door. Christ's resurrection is the title deed to life here and hereafter.

For the Christian, the final chapter of life does not close with the words, "the end." It is always "to be continued."

30. Is That Where We Are?

Now it came to pass that a group of poor, persecuted people left the shores of Europe for religious freedom in America. They were strangers and pilgrims, driven from place to place by their persecutors and suffering every kind of injustice and accusation. They moved at great risk of life.

Their love for God and for their fellowmen compelled them to speak out on behalf of justice for the poor and needy. Never would they own slaves. They witnessed against slavery when it meant suffering to do so. Furthermore they shared freely, as only the free and poor can share, from the depth of experience, feeling, and faith. A brother in need was a brother indeed.

As the Lord prospered these people in the land of plenty, it came to pass that they seemed to speak less and less for the poor and against injustice. With their mouths filled with food, their houses furnished with the finest, and their pockets packed with money, they found it difficult to speak against oppression or to plead for justice for all.

Behold now, sharing, when it was done at all, was done with little faith or feeling. It was shared out of plenty, not poverty; fullness, not faith; commandment, not compassion. The poor and oppressed were no longer brothers. They had become burdens — sometimes even opponents. Worst of all, the poor irritated the consciences of those who knew so well the Scripture which says that there is no faith or love if it doesn't lead one to respond to the need of others.

Therefore, instead of words of pity and petition on behalf of the needy, other expressions became common. Some said, "Anyone can get along if he only tries." Others said, "Look how I did it. If they would do like I did, they wouldn't be in the condition they are." Still others said, "Poor people are usually lazy people." Some even turned to ridicule by saying, "We fight poverty. We work."

With many other words the once poor, now wealthy and hardened people threw accusing and defaming remarks at the poor. For, lo, placing blame upon others is much easier than placing bread before them. Placing condemnation upon others is the old method of freeing ourselves from responsibility and obedience to God's commands. To brag of one's own accomplishments is older than Belshazzar who saw the handwriting on the wall.

Furthermore it is a great deal easier to cast blame on another than to help another to do better. The more we heap things to ourselves, the more also we heap threats at others.

Thus it also came to pass that cries for "law and order" were heard across the land. Those who had most cried loudest. They had so much to protect they were compelled to cry for law and order.

Their prayers for peace and quiet became loud and long in the midst of great upheaval. Those with plenty and peace are the ones who pray for peace and quiet. Such cry, "Peace, peace, when there is no peace." Those who are poor or downtrodden or suffer injustice can hardly be expected to pray for peace.

How different all was now for the children of those poor pilgrims who first came to

America for freedom. Before, others cried for them not to disturb the peace. Now they became the pleaders for peace. Before, others blamed them for destroying law and order. Now they became the blamers. Before, they were the derided poor. Now they became the deriders of the poor. For somewhere, someway, it all got turned around. And that's where we are now.

31. Enter as a Child

When we think of Jesus' statement about receiving the kingdom of God as a child does, we too often think only of such characteristics as dependence and need. But other characteristics of a child we need a great deal — such as, unrealized potential, openness to new ideas, complete confidence, and faith in the future.

A child has unrealized possibilities. So also in the kingdom into which we are born not as full-grown saints, but as God's dear children. Our potential is unlimited in Christ. Think again of the first disciples. Who in their day dreamed these poor persons would be about the only persons of their age to be remembered today? About the only other persons recalled today from their age are those who had some relationship to them or the kingdom they represented. So anyone who really receives the kingdom of God as they did has unrealized and unlimited potential. Paul, in Ephesians, says that God is just waiting to show forth the same power in us who believe, that He showed in Christ when He rasied Him from the dead.

In addition a child has openness to new ideas. As we become older we tend by nature to become status quo holders and staid. We become so set that it is difficult to convert persons over thirty on anything. But one of the things Christ does for a person who enters the kingdom in the spirit of a child is that He puts within such not only an openness to new light but also a great longing to know more and more new light. New ideas no longer frighten. Rather, an entire new life has begun and all things become new.

A child also lives with confidence. He trusts his parents and others completely, unless he has learned to mistrust because such have failed him. The child has little difficulty believing in the supernatural or that his needs will be provided for tomorrow. To enter the kingdom, therefore, as a child means to believe explicitly the promises of God. It is to have such confidence in Him for each tomorrow that come weal or woe, sunshine or shadow, nothing can happen outside His will. For, as Spurgeon one time said, "If we are in God's will, we are as safe here as in heaven itself."

Finally, a child faces the future in faith. A child does not dread tomorrow. The natural thing for a child is to be taken up with what is going on today. But he also always anticipates tomorrow. His hopes are high. To enter the kingdom as a child is to believe that God is as much the God of tomorrow as of yesterday and today. It is to work today with complete trust and rest, yet knowing that all the tomorrows will be brighter because under His rule and protection we will know Him better. His way will be clearer. We will understand ourselves better because He is in each tomorrow.

32. Make Love Your Aim

Too often we fail to look beneath the surface in our concern. We see actions or hear words and jump to conclusions which hurt rather than help persons. Christ calls us to transform all by love.

Paul, also in Philippians, prays that we may comprehend with all love. We never really understand a person until we love him. Love helps us see a person as he really is. Love changes our own viewpoint.

We forget that the person who acts condescendingly is likely painfully shy. Fighting the inward problem of shyness he seeks to hide it by standing aloof from persons or problems which would reveal his weakness. We look at his condescending attitude or aloofness and label him. Love leads us to accept him as he is. Since one does not need to hide anything in the presence of real love, help and insight are gained.

We forget that oftentimes the overcritical person is one starved for love and appreciation. This can happen at any age. The young person who does not experience the acceptance of love will likely become critical of anything which moves or doesn't move. He cannot get love and appreciation for being good; so he will get attention in some other way. Often this is by a very critical spirit.

The middle-aged person may basically act little different from the adolescent or teen-ager who seems against everything. We may see how such a person continually reacts, builds programs which center around himself, and condemns others in order to promote himself, yet fail to see that he is a person who needs love and appreciation rather than counter criticism.

A critical person desires love even though adolescent-like he may do the very things which make it harder to love him. The child who is love hungry will often do the very things for attention which cause people to love him less or even punish him. On the surface it may seem he wants to make parents or others angry with him. Deeper, however, is the desire to get attention and love.

Old age can be a trying time. Lifework and responsibility decrease. Others take over. We fail to continue to share words of love and appreciation for the contributions given even though small. What can easily happen in such a situation is that the person feels unwanted, unneeded, and unappreciated and he may take a critical stance against the church, society, or persons.

We forget that the noisy, aggressive youth is often sadly unsure of himself. So instead of encouraging him we may shove him on the sidelines or laugh at his antics. This causes even more insecurity. He feels no one else takes him seriously; so he becomes less and less sure of himself. Often a little confidence and love expressed can make the difference between failure and success in life. Love is quick to stand by the one who is shaky. Love can sense such a need long before life hits the rocks or falls.

No wonder Christ calls us to transform all by love. This begins by accepting people fully as they are, not as we wish they might be. One of our greatest faults is that we want to love people the way we wish they were rather than the way they are. Love loves people just as they are. Love comprehends the possibilities which lie beneath the surface. Nothing so much changes our own attitudes as love. Nothing so much changes other people as love. Nothing else so much outlasts life itself. Therefore as the Apostle Paul says, "Make love your aim."

33. Wind of the Spirit, Blow

A friend and I were walking the streets of Jerusalem late one night. We had visited shrine after shrine during the day. Here in the heart of three great religions, we saw some of the most sincere worshipers we had ever seen. Suddenly my friend turned to me and said, "You know, only a mighty work of the Holy Spirit can break through all which keeps people in the Holy Land from really seeing Christ. If much of what we see here is supposed to be Christianity, then it is understandable that folks do not accept it."

"But," I said, "it is no more true here in the Holy Land than anywhere else. At home also it will take the wind of the Spirit to blow away all the unworthy accretions which Christianity has gathered before people will be able to see the true essence of the gospel in Christ."

If Christianity is merely monuments and sacred shrines which point to the past, then it is as dead as any other faith. True, Christianity is historical. True, it has a great and glorious past. But if that same Christ who was known by those early disciples is not known by us, we are of all men most miserable. If that same Holy Spirit which baptized those early believers has not baptized us, we are as helpless as they were before Pentecost.

Yes, I have long ago concluded that only a great outpouring of the Holy Spirit which demonstrates again the supernatural character of the Christian faith will crack the crust of deadness in what is today a cold and calloused Christianity in so many places and in so many lives.

We are too often like the disciples in the valley who could not help the needy father and his son. There was help, however. Suddenly, when they saw their own failure and inadequacy, they looked up and saw Jesus coming down the hill toward them. Turning to the troubled father they said, "Man, we cannot do what is needed. But here comes Jesus. He can do anything." This second step is the step so much needed today. After recognizing our own inadequacy we must take the step of simple faith, which will not stagger at the promises of God, and turn the eyes of people to Christ. This is the Spirit's work. He shall not speak of Himself but He shall speak of Christ.

This is why the Spirit is sent — to reveal Christ as He really is and to change us into His same image. How we need His ministry today! People will never really be impressed for God by beautiful buildings and by lives which merely refrain from doing things which others do. There is an abundance of these in every part of the world. The world is struck for God when, by the power of His Holy Spirit, His people are enabled to live beautiful supernatural lives which the world admits it cannot match.

If it is true that only a fresh pouring out of God's Spirit will reveal Christ and make the Word flesh under the secular attack of today, then we must be open to the Spirit whenever and in whatever way He wishes to come. We dare not set up our requirements for the Spirit's work. He sets up His own. We dare not say He must follow a prescribed formula and form. Read Acts and you see Him working in many different ways and through many different people. Our responsibility is to be honestly open to His work in our own lives. We must trust Him to work in the lives of other believers.

Without telling what or how the Spirit should work, we do know from the Scriptures that three things will be true in a Spirit-led work. First, the Spirit's work is to magnify Jesus Christ. Those in whom He works will love Jesus Christ more. They will not speak of themselves, even as the Spirit speaks not of Himself. But they will speak for Jesus Christ.

Second, a work of the Spirit will magnify the Word of God. He will create love for the Word which means a love not only to hear but to obey. The Holy Spirit is given, in the final analysis, only to "them that obey him."

Third, a work of the Holy Spirit will produce the fruit of the Spirit. The great work of the Spirit, which preceded and produced the Welsh revival and reached around the globe, was such a manifestation of the fruit of love, joy, and peace and the rest of the fruit of the Spirit that the unsaved and unsanctified cried out in repentance and faith.

34. Audacity to Believe the Gospel

In his review of John R. W. Stott's recent book, *One People*, D. Elton Trueblood makes some interesting comments concerning the ministry of Stott. Trueblood tells how, while living in England, he looked for signs of hope in the Christian movement. Although hope was hard to find, he did find one which was encouraging. It was in the work and ministry of John Stott, rector of All Souls Church, Langham Place, London.

Trueblood said, "Noting that most church buildings were relatively empty, even on Sunday morning, someone suggested that we try All Souls. To our amazement, when we reached there Sunday evening, we had difficulty in finding seats in the large building which provides a dramatic termination to Regent Street.

"The balcony, as well as the main part of the church building, was filled and, what was even more remarkable, it was obvious that at least half of the worshipers were under the age of twenty-five. Naturally we listened carefully to see what John Stott said and which other preachers lacked. . . .

"We found he differed from others simply in the fact that he had an affirmative message to proclaim. He did not merely give back the problems to those looking for answers. He stood out as almost an oddity in the London scene because he had the audacity to believe the gospel."

After hearing Stott preach several years ago, and now again after reading Trueblood's statement, my heart cries out, "God, give us more preachers like that. Give us preachers who have the audacity to believe and preach the gospel."

As I listened to Stott at the Berlin Congress on Evangelism, I was deeply moved by the effectiveness of the gospel presented in a clear way, without all kinds of human rationalizations, qualifications, and judgments. Here was no preacher bemoaning the times. He was discerning the times. Here was no prophet of doom. He was a prophet of hope. Here was no little person seeking to picture the faults of others. Stott was a preacher of Christ in all His greatness and glory.

A preacher who has the audacity to believe the gospel finds that it "is the power of God unto salvation." Christ is still saying, "And I, if I be lifted up from the earth, will draw all men unto me."

Today our youth are saying they are sick of religion. But they declare with equal vigor they are excited about Jesus Christ. The problem is that He is so seldom presented. Church problems, personal problems, and political problems are preached to the exclusion of Christ. Until Christ is preached, there really aren't any true answers.

When a preacher has the audacity to believe the gospel, Christ is made unto him wisdom and righteousness. Man is not converted by our great thoughts and human wisdom but by the person Jesus Christ and the power of His Holy Spirit.

Today, when our world is flooded with wisdom and knowledge as never before, we are told we are merely producing the most educated sinners ever. People remain sinners because human wisdom and intellectuality, no matter how great, cannot redeem. Until Christ is preached, and we realize that human wisdom has absolutely no power or ability to work spiritual change, there will be no hope.

When we have the audacity to believe the gospel and believe that this takes precedence over the precepts and traditions of man, then will we have a message to answer the cries of our age. This belief will drive us to a thorough study of the Scriptures. It will enable us to speak with authority and not as the scribes. Then also we will have a message the Holy Spirit can use, for God cannot bless a mere human message no matter how eloquent or thought-provoking.

Thank God for the growing number who have the audacity to believe the gospel. May the number of those who walk in such simple faith increase. Then shall be brought to pass the prophecy that God's Spirit shall be poured out in ways underdreamed of in these last days. We shall pray to this end.

35. The Muckraker–
A Successful Failure

John Bunyan in his classic *Pilgrim's Progress* describes the man with a muckracke in his hand. He could "look no way but downwards." Although one stood over him offering him a celestial crown, the muckraker did not look up but continued to rake to himself the straws, the small sticks, and dust off the floor. Bunyan says this shows his carnal mind.

All of us must beware of muckraking. Bunyan referred to muck as earthly things in contrast to eternal or heavenly things. Muck is usually defined today as anything which injures or tends to injure the reputation or standing of another. It may be truth but truth publicized to hurt another. Thus a muckraker is one who searches out and seeks to expose publicly real or apparent misconduct and failing on the part of another (usually a leader).

Today muckraking seems popular. Some even attempt to prove their own orthodoxy by digging up the muck in other people's lives. It probably, as Bunyan says, "shows the carnal mind."

But even the most successful muckraker is a complete failure in the end because he finally concludes his lifework with only a pile of dirt. He uses his hours and days searching out that which injures instead of helps. Muckraking still has its first soul to win for the right and its first soul to keep from the wrong.

So it is that writers, preachers, teachers, parents, really all of us, must beware of being muckrakers. Following is a parable which may serve as warning to us all.

Now it came to pass on a certain day a man set out to find muck. And lo, he was exceedingly successful. From the start he found plenty of assistance. Muck is everywhere people live and thus it did not take sharp eyesight or insight to find it. The man's aim was to collect it and pile it as high as he could.

In his search for muck he dug into the

writings and lives of small and great. And behold he found that all made mistakes in judgment and thought. As in even the grandest house some dust is seen, so also in the grandest life some muck can be sighted. Abraham lied, Jacob deceived. Thomas doubted, Peter denied, Moses became angry, and lo, even Noah, the first man called righteous by God, was guilty of immorality.

Thus this man decided to limit his search for muck to the living, even those of his own brethren. And behold he found much muck, for he picked out each picayune word and phrase which "perhaps" pointed to some muck.

Straightway his pile of muck became higher and higher. Because his business grew so rapidly and others liked the muck, he gave much time to finding more. Muckraking became his major work.

When it was still a small pile, some thought he dug for and discovered gold. But when the pile became large, more and more understood it was only muck he was piling up.

Now it came to pass that in his finding of muck none escaped his scrutinizing eye. Only he himself was safe. For he had an eye to see muck everywhere. Thus even those who

144

were his best helpers at first gradually slunk away until the man was left alone to his muckraking.

But still he kept at it. In fact, now he developed a religious fervor about it all. People must be made to see muck. People must be saved from muck even if they never imagined it existed. So he sent samples all over the land. He spoke of muck on radio. He described muck in literature. And he put his muck on public display with a large sign, "Learn more about muck."

Now behold, as the muck pile became higher and higher, a long shadow fell around. The higher the muck pile became, the more the sun was shut out. For the man who raked muck· was shutting out light. His interest was muck, not light.

His eyes did not see the gathering darkness, for his eyes became accustomed to the dark. Finally he found he could gather muck best in the dark. And behold he had built a mountain of muck around so that he himself could no longer look or climb over it. Furthermore, he never lifted his eyes from the ground.

Now it came to pass that the muckraker became old. He had many fears. He ached from muck disease. For life was almost over and

145

lo, all he had accomplished was gathering a large pile of muck. His life was wasted on this.

When he died, folks who couldn't remember his name simply said, "Behold, the muckraker is dead."

Thereafter, when anyone inquired about the meaning of the pile of muck, people answered, "That pile of muck was gathered by a man who spent his life raking muck." The muck remained, but the man was simply called the muckraker.

36. We Are Strange Creatures

We want something; so we pretend to purchase it for the children.

We feel bad about something we did or did not do and so we take our frustrations out on our children, other people, or the church.

We speak of the power of pictures which leave such deep impressions because they combine the ear and eye gate for learning. Then we seek to persuade ourselves that savagery, killing, and immodesty on the TV or movie have no harmful effect on our children.

We drive an expensive "heavier" car because we say "we travel a great deal or we cannot stand the vibrations." But after we pull the car into the garage, we climb on a luxurious vibrating chair or mattress.

We are desirous of buying a new appliance or car. In order to justify the purchase we seek to find some flaw to get rid of our present model. But when we sell the old model, we imply it is in perfect shape.

We speak of the sin of taking the Bible and prayer out of our public schools but seldom read our Bibles or pray with our families.

We wax eloquent on the corruption of communism because, we say, it compels people to cease attending church, reading the Bible, and giving open testimony for Christ. But what the communists do by force, we do by choice.

We are quick to tell people that we belong to the church. But when there is work to do, we say, "Let them do it." Or when something goes wrong, we say, "They are responsible." We even blame "the church" for not taking a stand or failing in its task. But who is the church?

We deplore juvenile delinquency and lawlessness in our society. Then we take our children into our cars and exceed the speed limit, do not stop at stop signs, and boast over the dinner table how we were caught for breaking the law but cleverly escaped a fine.

We cheat on income tax forms and deplore the young person who cheats on his school exams.

We are strange creatures.

37. Churches, Clergy, and Convenience

We are told that two prevalent questions people ask today when choosing a church to join are: "What kind of preacher do they have?" and "Do they have a parking lot?"

I think these are important questions, don't you? It's important what kind of preacher I listen to, isn't it? And, when I go to church, I want to park, that is, I don't like to drive all over town hunting a place to put the car and then walk one or more blocks to church.

These questions can be answered quickly. However, I'm made to think there's something else behind such questions. I'm not sure of course. Several ideas come to my mind.

What do we really think of when we think of church?

Our age is saturated with hero worshipers. We love superlatives. We've developed a certain kind of person cult. He's the best preacher. He's the most powerful preacher. He's the best person for the youth of the church. Do we promote the spirit of "having . . . persons in admiration"?

We may come close to the carnal Corinthian spirit which expressed itself in "I'm for Apollos — he's the most eloquent preacher; I'm for Peter — he's the most straightforward speaker; I'm for Paul — he's the best theologian and organizational man."

We need to see again that to join a church with the greatest preacher doesn't guarantee glory. To glory in man more than God merely means idol worship.

Yes, certainly, I'm all for proper respect, reverence, and honor for the minister of God. Most places he deserves more than he's receiving. But that's not the point here. The point is that we don't go to church to worship the preacher, to please the preacher, or to be pleased by him. We go to worship God, to hear Him speak, and to fellowship with His people. We go to worship God, obey Him, be strengthened by Him, and go forth to serve more faithfully.

How about the second question: "Do they have a parking lot?" For one thing it may say something to those planning to build a new church. Plan for a parking lot. That is what people are asking about.

Beyond this, the question may dramatize our desire for and love of convenience these days. In our homes, on our jobs, even in our play, there must be convenience. And, of course, our religion dare offer no inconvenience or we're just not interested. We are willing to do a little toward satisfying our conscience when it comes to going to church, but when it's inconvenient, it's out. We need our recreation, relaxation, and visitation. God forbid that our religion should infringe on these. In fact, one is made to feel that we desire a religion that does not infringe on our sin, self, or Sunday plans.

And may God pardon us. He knows we mean well. He knows how we must put up with inconvenience when we go shopping and sight-seeing. We are worn out till that is done. He doesn't want or expect us to let anything in our religion bring added bother or burden, does He?

May God help us! Such religion is entirely satisfactory to the devil himself. We aren't kidding God. He knows that no ball game is rained or snowed out as easily as a church service or spiritual function. Nineteen drops of water will keep twenty people away from nearly any service.

And God knows the effort we put into getting off to a vacation. He knows the inconvenience endured to get that special advertised bargain we saw in the paper.

Mind you, God may not even care if a church has a parking lot or not. He is concerned about some other things. He is, as always, interested in those who will put His work first, even to the cost of not only inconvenience but death itself. He says He is still seeking those who "worship him in spirit and in truth." He never has taken second place, and, put it down, He won't!

I believe that rather than asking who is the preacher, we ought to be crying out for communion with God and His people, and "so much the more, as . . .[we] see the day approaching." We ought to be thanking God that we still have the opportunity and privilege of united worship in His name with freedom and favor.

Perhaps by now you are saying, "Well, he's writing all this on a blue Monday. He's

153

worked up over a few incidentals." The fact is that I'm writing this the day after Christmas. I'm writing this out of the Christmas context which calls us as Christians to join in praise and adoration to God and which clearly points all of us to the complete claims of Christ for every life.

It's in this context of heaven's hosts praising God and men of old giving their best that I write.

In the midst of the true meaning of Christmas, we must confess that too often we put our faith in man before God and so praise men more than God. In the context of Christmas, we confess that we find ourselves too often putting convenience before Christ, who chose the way of the manger, the wilderness, and the cross.

38. What Concerns Us?

At the beginning of the Bolshevik revolution two meetings took place simultaneously on the same Moscow street. The leaders of the revolution met in one house. In the other the leaders of the Orthodox Church were gathered.

The first meeting concerned itself with plans that were to change the course of modern history, while the second was locked in an intense discussion regarding proposed changes in the color of vestments. Thus a church once virile and aggressive had settled down to insignificant issues. When its witness was most needed, its houses of worship were turned into museums and its witness was dissipated by debate.

In a particular way our day is a day of

destiny. Even a casual observer can see it as a day of unparalleled opportunity and urgency. This, of course, makes it also a day of decision.

Today we are at the beginning of a new era. This means that what is done now determines the direction for years to come. Will we concentrate on the secondary and be merely another anonymous voice amid a clamor of conflicting opinions or will we possess the precious moments to present Christ to the world?

Of course we can hide behind the walls of beautiful sanctuaries and forget the needs, cries, and unending heartbreak of the world. But if we are to be Christians today, we will not conclude our service on Sunday in a beautiful sanctuary, but we will carry our commitment to Christ and the compassion of Christ to the people in the marketplace.

Two sins seem to shadow much of church history: one is the Christian's struggle for respectability and the other is the Christian's gradual loss of an evangelistic spirit. When we struggle to be well thought of more than to be true to Christ, we lose our power and penetration. When we lose our evangelistic fervor, we are dead and deserve burial.

156

39. Let Us Affirm Our Faith

I suggest that we are at the time when we
must stop analyzing and criticizing the Christian faith and start affirming it. For long
enough the church has looked at itself, talked
against itself, lambasted itself, and stressed
what it cannot do and cannot believe. It is
passing through what might correctly be
called the age of negation. This age started
with the development of long lists of "do's"
and don'ts." Then the church started to
criticize this approach. And it seems the church
never pulled out of this position of critic "par
excellence."

Now, by all appearances, people are tired,
very tired of the negative, critical approach to
the church situation. Many members have

left already. Others promise to quit unless the climate is changed. Many young people have believed what the church says about itself. They also have left or are nauseated. Louis Cassels sounds right when he writes what he believes is the most important reason why people are drifting away from the church: "They haven't found in the church what they hoped to find — a confident faith in God."

A confident faith can hardly be expected in the presence of a defeatist, antagonistic, and critical spirit. Neither can it be found where there is continual analysis. This only produces, as someone suggested, the "paralysis of analysis." The church has spent too much time analyzing the predicament until it becomes annoying like the old lady who is forever sharing all her ailments. Analysis has its place. But it should not be primary.

The Scripture stresses the exodus of sin more than the genesis of sin. It says more about God's forgiveness of sin than man's fall into sin.

George MacDonald says, "Analysis is well, as death is well." Dead bodies are dissected and studied. No amount of examining, measuring, and analyzing can give life. Wadsworth wrote, "To dissect is to kill."

Wilfred Reynolds makes a sobering statement: "A sure sign that a religious group has all but lost its way is when the corporate body is confused about role, direction, and identity. A preoccupation with analysis, evaluation, and guidelines is symptomatic of the spontaneity and fire being mostly nonexistent."

An educational leader said that a typical discussion on any college campus is likely to be on love or religion. But too often it is religion being analyzed and debated rather than religion as a matter of joyful confidence and song.

Many church leaders can be held responsible for the negative attitude toward the church. During the last decade the church was scolded much more than shepherded. It was chided much more than cared for. It was moaned about much more than ministered to.

Any other body would have died years ago from such treatment. Name any other work which could have persisted with so high a percentage of its managers and members pointing out its failures while doing so little to present a positive position.

But church leaders also suffered severe handicap in the criticism. Ministers were told of their complete incompetence. They were told that their work is no longer valid, preaching belongs to the past, and their message is irrelevant for today.

Church members were told they come to church for the wrong reasons, give with the wrong motives, and represent the wrong things to the world. For fellowship the beer hall was at times recommended over the church. All these things and many more were said by members of the church with almost nothing said as to what it means to minister, and what a vital Christian life or congregation is.

Today is the time to move beyond these morose descriptions of the church. We want to be told what we *can* believe. We want to know what the church can affirm rather than what it can no longer believe. We are tired of hearing leaders with all kinds of reservations.

We are seeing that the doubters have little to offer. The skeptics have spoken their piece without strengthening any cause. As one spiritual leader said years ago, "Any fool can knock props out from under a cripple. It takes some sincere concern and thought to put props under."

And we are all at least in some sense cripples. We need each other and the help each can give rather than being told all the time that we are cripples. This means, for one thing, that in the church's concern for the social, the inner-city, the racial problems in the world, we dare not forget that each congregation also has real burning needs to be ministered to.

Without a doubt it's time the church — that is, you and I — must declare what it believes — not in a dogmatic, domineering, and bigoted way, but in a radiant, ready, and buoyant way. Christianity is not dependent upon discussion or debate but upon declaration by word and work.

Perhaps it is past due for all of us to again write down what we believe and say it so that people know. Perhaps the season is ripe for every Sunday school teacher to say clearly what he affirms. I've heard some teachers raise only doubts. Perhaps the moment is here for every member to write for the record what he will live and die for. Such exercise probably would bring revival. Revival involves not only confession and repentance but also the affirmation of faith.

161

40. A Pilgrim's Path

Someone said the church so easily moves from a tent to a temple to a tomb. Like Abraham, the church responds to the call of faith to move out not knowing where such a dedication will lead. It constantly reminds itself that it is a sojourner, a pilgrim, and does not allow itself to be tied down too hard — for a while.

After a while the pilgrim life seems so hard and the way of the world seems so delightful. In adapting here and there the church finds life somewhat smooth and it says, "Let us build our tabernacles here." So it begins to build big cathedrals and the Dark Ages are upon it.

Yes, it always draws me up short when I see

Christians putting their millions in brick and mortar because I remember history which says the cathedrals were built during the Dark Ages. I remember that when the church is nearly dead it seems to seek to demonstrate to people that it is alive by doing some great external thing which people can see. And this is done primarily for "itself" instead of bringing blessing to others.

At this stage also a great deal of time is spent on the kind and color of the vestments and the care of the church's investments. The church needs little or nothing. The pilgrims are become princes. Faith seems less needed than finances. And prayer seems secondary to program.

Now the next step is a natural one. The church says, "Let us die here." Here is where our fathers lived. And here is where we were brought up. And here is where we have built these great buildings. Let us also build our tombs here. This is a good land in which to die. For now the pilgrims are become princes who plan their pyramids for the great dead. Yes, the church has moved from a tent to a temple to a tomb.

Sometimes it seems that the church of today may be nearer than it realizes to turn again to tents, to the walk of faith, the pilgrim path. Perhaps persecution is not far away.

Perhaps in our own lifetime the church may again be driven into the dens and God will, out of His great love, allow our possessions to be taken from us so that we might be better able to walk by faith, so that we might know the preciousness of the pilgrim path.

Perhaps 1 Peter will again be one of the most read books of the New Testament, for it pictures for us so majestically the pilgrim's path through the wilderness of this world to the next. It has always been a favorite for pilgrims.

41. What Does God Say?

Some time ago I attended a meeting in which great speeches were spoken. Great papers were presented. Great responses were given. Many excellent insights were shared. Nothing was proposed which sanctioned wrong-doing as far as I could discern. Some weaknesses and some strengths of the church were called to attention. Several good suggestions were given for improvement.

At the close of this two-day meeting one of the great spiritual leaders of the past several generations shared with me an observation. I've pondered it many times since. "It seems to me," he said, "that our forefathers would have used some Scripture in such discussions to help us know what God says on the subject."

165

Here is a growing weakness in church, family, and individual life. Too many discussions include only what we think. Even some preaching is simply the propounding of another philosophical idea. Exposition of the Scripture may be at an all-time low for this century in certain pulpits while people inwardly crave spiritual food. God, through Jeremiah, has seven statements concerning the spiritual leaders of that day. One has to do with pastors who do not feed the flock but follow many fancies and philosophies of their day.

But we in general seem to take less time with the Scripture. We blame the preacher for not feeding us, yet we do not eat at home. Few, if any, could survive physically if we ate only once or twice a week. And it would sound insane to blame a person who invites us to a meal on Sunday for not feeding us enough for all week, if we ate nothing the other six days. Yet there are those who do not study the Scripture all week and yet complain that they are not fed enough on Sunday morning. What this says is that the obligation for spiritual nourishment is on all, the individual Christian, the body of believers, and the spiritual leaders.

Are we asking what God has to say about

the common concerns? In the past no doubt we tried to settle matters by citing a quick proof text and making it absolute — no gold, no movies, no dancing, etc. This approach sometimes closed all discussion and cut off any who differed. No doubt also sometimes our Bibles became clubs to fight any who did not agree with us.

Then, because changes came and we felt we could not be so absolute in some things, we began to speak of holding to the overall principles. Certainly this was better. However, the danger now is that, in many discussions, not even the principles of the Scripture are cited. Discussions are held and decisions are made with little or no reference to what God has to say. At times one may even feel sort of naive when he says, "But the Bible says. . . ."

Yet the fact remains that our forefathers cared little about any decision which did not draw its conclusions from the Scripture. Their belief was that if the Scripture said it, then it is to be followed. Christ was Lord of life and His whisper was to be obeyed above the words of the world. Christ's call was above the cries of the crowd.

True, the brotherhood, guided by the Holy Spirit, was important in making decisions. Yet the Scriptures were central in consultation. Brothers were bound together to live in the light of the Bible as they understood it, always searching for more illumination.

So a mere discussion of current events is not enough. Neither will new nor old philosophies do. Nothing will satisfy until followers of Christ determine to obey the gospel. And to obey the gospel means to know what it is about. Therefore the gospel must be central in all our life and discussions. Else we will become increasingly biblically illiterate and spiritually at sea.

Even the Holy Spirit is helpless to do a spiritual work until the Word is presented. The Holy Spirit uses the Scripture to convict and convince. Until the Word is shared the Holy Spirit cannot use that Word to meet the needs of man. Until the Scripture is studied the church or individual cannot receive spiritual illumination or truth to share.

The time is ripe for a fresh concern with what God has to say in His Word. Pastors ought always to be declaring what God says on the issues of today. Congregations must be discussing present problems in the light of the Scripture. The old title used for many sermons and studies, "What the Bible Says

About. . . ," was a rather good way of putting it. And one has a feeling that such topics might pick up a great deal of interest where persons are weary of discussions in which personal opinions are hashed over again and again. Down deep, if we are at all serious about being Christian, we want to know, What does God say?

42. Needed–Flexibility and Depth

Different words describe our day. With footprints on the face of the moon we now know for sure we are in the space age. Never before has so much been put into so single an effort. Turmoil at every turn tells us we are in a time of crisis. Never before have life and death issues cut across so many structures of society and been so wide in scope. The degree to which the church can act in crisis determines the degree to which it can be an instrument of redemption.

To meet the days ahead two things are desperately needed. We will need a flexibility and a depth far greater than we now experience.

Like any institution of age the church tends

170

to be inflexible. It is inclined to operate more from memory and habit than from imagination and daring. It loves to be safe. It tends to be committed to past programs, activities, and goals. These seem more secure. Security has always been dangerous for the church.

So as the church moves from one age to another, its flexibility, its ability to meet the new, is tested. The Renaissance demanded a Reformation. The established church was too immovable. In the emergence of the industrial age, men moved by the Spirit saw the demands of the new day and were used by God to free many from the inflexible character the church had developed. There was a freedom to live and share the gospel. Again in the technological age the church is moved to grasp new means of sharing the gospel.

Today also demands great imagination and daring. We must somehow learn to discern what is basic, essential, and creative if we are to be the church. If we are to meet the needs of the space age, we must have quick adaptability. If we cannot meet people Sunday morning, we must meet them on Monday morning. We will need to find new ways to take the gospel into the highways, byways, and skyways. If we do not, we will be only ordained echoes mouthing cliches of uninformed theology and playing church like children who do not realize the responsibilities of real and living faith.

Someone cuttingly quipped about the famous old church in London, which surveyors discovered to be moving down Fleet Street at the rate of an inch each one hundred years: "Anyone can see that a church ought to be able to travel a little faster than that."

This means that no program or building or organization dare be so sacred it stops us from sharing the gospel. The traditional religious patterns of life will be tested. Crisis in every area, as well as mobility of our population, long weekends, extended vacations, urban life, will demand a sensitivity to the Spirit and the flexibility only He can give in meeting the new situation for Christ.

A new depth is also needed — a depth of commitment to Christ the Captain of our salvation and to the word of His command. As one writer put it, "The forecast is for rough seas and unfavorable winds." Who does not sense the truth of this?

On these rough seas some of the crew are threatening to desert. Some are confused as to the course. Many are in too shallow water and too narrow channels. Even mutiny is threatening at times.

The church will need to travel light if it is to be responsive to the Spirit. Perhaps it will need to throw overboard much of what it thought was precious cargo. But this is not the first time this has happened.

John Zercher, editor of *Evangelical Visitor*, says, "The spirit of the years ahead will militate against the nominal church member. We will be driven again to a believers' church. Social prestige for belonging to the church is past. Family or church tradition is of little account to many. The church of the future will be a committed church or it will not stand the stress." After all, what's the use of gadgets, status, position, organization, brick and mortar if the reason for living is lost?

During the past dozen or so decades the church in America has had it rather calm. The times were kind as a whole and did little to test faith. The church which ought to be the greatest shaker of the "status quo" lost desire for the distinctly different life.

Today is difficult. The foundations of faith are shaken. The lack of conviction on the part of the church is suddenly seen when it's compared to the conviction of those who take up opposing causes with a dedication to the death.

If people are to pay attention to our preaching, our text today must be from the "exemplified version." People long to look as well as listen. The works of our lives must conform to the words of our lips. We must put our heart where our mouth is or stop claiming to be Christians.

I'm persuaded that true religion is not being destroyed in our time. But bad religion is being brought under judgment. Christianity is not being discarded but institutionally pretentious Christendom is being rocked to the foundations. In the words of Hebrews, God is shaking the things which can be shaken so that we might see the things which remain. May God help us see the things which are eternal!

When the Christian is close to his Lord, he is not a peddler of pessimism. Neither is he an idolater of the past, praising yesterday's faithful living. He is God's answer for each new day which dawns.